THE SCROLLS OF
BELBOU

THE SCROLLS OF
BELBOU

One Boy's Duty, a Continent's Fate

DMITRI TOUL

ARPress
ILLUMINATING IDEAS.
EMPOWERING VOICES

ARPress
45 Dan Road Suite 15
Canton, MA 02021

Hotline: 1(888) 821-0229
Fax: 1(508) 545-7580

Ordering Information:
Quantity sales. Special discounts are available on quantity purchases by corporations,associations, and others. For details, contact the publisher at the address above.

Printed in the United States of America.

ISBN-13:   Softcover   979-8-89676-177-8
             eBook   979-8-89676-178-5

Library of Congress Control Number: 2025913053

TABLE OF CONTENTS

THE ISLANDS

On the continent was where life hummed along, and its masses of people carried on the day to day business of life sharing activities. The other areas of the world sustained it, areas where inhabitation was minimal and living conditions crude and poor at best. From these areas men would venture out to mine and cultivate, but never to live, for the continent was home and there they were content.

A chain of islands was situated about forty kilometers away off the western coast of the continent. Some could support life if hard work was maintained, while others were just lonely mounds protruding out of the sea. History was not kind to these islands. Very little was known of their past, and most exploration proved fruitless in providing any importance to the main. Legend had it that from these islands came a great people who had purged the continent of an evil force. These people lived on these islands and were governed by great kings, and the kings lived and ruled from one island in particular. Its name was Eden.

But as legends are stories passed on from generation to generation, usually some historical fact will give some credence to them. However, no evidence could be found to back this legend, and so as the legend faintly lived, it gave a beautiful story, but was not given much true interest by most men of the sciences.

On the island there lives today a group of stouthearted people who seemed uncommonly independent, and though they would visit the continent, would always return. They were mostly coastal dwellers, fishermen by main trade, and some were wood carvers, developers of exquisite and intricate sculpture that was in great demand on the main.

These people were of high intelligence, and yet they had no known record, nor could they tell how long their ancestors had been there. All they knew was their race had inhabited the islands since the beginning of time. They were a proud people, ones who knew of the legends, too. But even they could not substantiate the stories of long ago.

The last census from the mainland was not exact, but it was still accurate enough for the ruling government. It placed the islanders at about seventeen hundred inhabitants, with about twelve hundred and fifty living on the island called Mylako. They were a close knit society which carried on constant visitation by each other from island to island, but Mylako was the base, and it is from here that our story comes.

Often during the summer and fall periods, tourists would visit the islands. But the natives of Mylako were responsible for having the continent's government restrain the number of people who could visit, and because of this order, only a few wanted to go through the necessary channels. Those who did stop on the islands were treated cordially and pleasantly.

The restrictions were placed on the continent's main subjects many years ago to preserve the ethnic quality of the islands, ensure the continual quality of the workmanship of the desired tradesmen. And to prevent any turmoil over possible annexation of the island's society, though harmonious to outsiders, these locked out any aspirations for the mainland's inhabitants to live there. Anyone was free to leave the islands to live elsewhere, but outsiders were not able to leave the main to become part of the islands. This unwritten and nonverbal precept over time permeated both sides of the lands; and so without thinking or feeling on either side, this "law" was observed.

And it was without ill feeling that the islanders allowed the continent to rule over them. As mentioned in years gone by, as long as separation was endured, the islanders permitted government from abroad. They had no real leaders, and no one could remember self rule in recent past. Thus, this coexistence proved decent and profitable for both people.

To get to the island, though only forty kilometers from the closest harbor, sometimes proved tricky and dangerous. The channel currents often proved too strong for smooth and quick passage, and often unexpected storms lashed out, causing even the most seasoned pilot to fear crossing. With suddenness, unexplained winds would whip the ships about and waves would crash with dangerous fury upon even the stoutest ship. And then just as suddenly all would cease and quiet and calm would prevail.

Because of this, most passage between the Confederacy, which made up the continental makeup and Mylako would be by airships. These dirigibles allowed for much safer and constant travel. Hot air ballooning was invented years earlier, but airships were relatively new being put into regular use for about twenty years. Its creativity opened up new scopes of discovery, and even the continent itself was being remapped, and previous knowledge of it being contested in the scientific courts of the Confederacy.

Bold men, courageous and curious, had already ventured far eastward into the state of Froth, and government sponsored voyages of around the globe were in the planning. One such trip over Mylako on a pre-surveying mission was blown off course from the coastline towards the northwest area of its great forest. So thickly wooded was this forest that previous views of it seemed to be one of a great mass of impregnable green. But the same storms that lashed the islands the day before caused in its residue winds that carried the airship Quester off its course.

Below, after the storm, the forest looked like a mass of unkempt hair, frazzled and shaken. As they passed over, quickly the map man sketched the disheveled view before him, thinking nothing of the scene, but only to hasten his work. It would take months of regular coastline mapping before the Quester could move inland, and this strange scene seemed too original to pass up. Where the mass was once as one, there appeared an area several meters more opened than normal and a solid item also seemed present. Marking the view on the quadrant, the map man continued hastily to proceed further in his sketching.

Bob Troyer was finishing up the report he was working on concerning the eastern section of the Confederacy, and that was the state of Froth. He had spent many weeks gathering information on that part of the continent and probably only Mr. Moriarity, the government's top advisor on historical and human affairs knew more than he did about Froth. Anthropology was a career few students cared to know about, but Bob loved his work, and looked forward to the upcoming expedition into that part of the land where even today most people mysteriously shunned.

It was the end of summer and soon his children would have to go back to school. To combine work and play was one serendipity of his field, and a two-week field trip with his family was coming up in two days.

"Bob!" Mr. Moriarity called out. "Before you leave, please come here for a few minutes."

Stacking the reports neatly in the bin where he could look at them after vacation, he entered Mr. Moriarity's office next door. The professor was bent over the table and looking at some papers through his ever-present magnifying glass.

"I just received these papers from the airship Quester this morning. No one mentioned anything out of the ordinary except for being blown off course, but look at this one sketch and see if you see anything strange about it."

"There seems to be an open area in quadrant 117. I wonder why he drew a rectangle in it, too?" Bob said. "We both walked that coastline before, and only you did any penetration of the forest. Did you ever encounter an opening like this?"

"Not likely, Bob. Besides, I went only about a mile into it. I'm not a young man, and it wasn't too long ago that I did it. That forest is just so damn thick with growth. Only by the airships have we been able to see the whole thing."

"Holy Moses, Bob!" As Moriarity's hands seemed to shake. "You know how I feel about those islands. I've been spending a lifetime aching to know what its history consist of and to give backbone to the legends."

"Ah yes! The legends of the islands." Bob murmured. "It's hard not to like the story of good over evil. After all, isn't every fairy tale composed of such a theme?"

"Fairy tale in a pig's eye, Bob!" shouted Moriarity. "I truly feel something marvelous happened years ago that shaped our destiny. Mercy! How do you explain the eerie feelings people still feel about Froth? Are you still going to take Nance, Roger, and Sally with you?"

"Take it easy old friend," Bob chuckled. "I didn't mean to ridicule you. And I feel safe about this trip. No reports of danger have come out of Froth in my lifetime."

"Yes, of course." bellowed Mr. Moriarity. "But when I went on an expedition there, I never went as deep as to where the airship will take you. Bob, listen, I have a tremendous favor to ask you, and no ill feelings if you turn it down."

Bob could sense the excitement and yet the concern in his friend's voice and manner. The years working together had meant so much to him, and fondly he knew to the professor, also. "Ask, and almost certainly it is yours."

"Bob," Moriarity sighed as he sat down. "I want you to change your plans and safari to that quadrant on Mylako. I would go, God only knows how much I dream of going, but you are my only ears and eyes. I've arranged a five-day excursion to the islands. I know it's not much time, but it's all I could get the university to pay for on such short notice. But we could be on to something here. I'm counting on you, Bob, but by not going to Froth, they will save money, also. I know your trip took some time to get all the necessary forms and permission from the government. I also know you'll lose the expedition to Froth should you do me this favor. Others could go, but, well, you are like my right arm. You think like me and feel like me. Our work is like a child to us."

"Whew! This is so sudden."

"I know, but don't worry. In the spring I'll arrange another expedition to Froth for you. Go where I cannot go and see what I have longed to see. Bring back my legend to me."

Bob looked into the old man's eyes. Always so conservative and thorough, and now over a piece of sketching acting like a novice. The professor appeared childlike in his request. "I'll tell Nance we go west as soon as I get home."

"And I'll have all the supplies and equipment you'll need for the trip. Just show up at the air dock and everything will be taken care of for you."

"What if, what if we find nothing, professor?" Bob stammered.

"Because it is you, Bob, and no one else going, I guess I can accept the ancient stories as legends. But I have thought on this, too." As Moriarity's eyes twinkled. "Don't think me too foolish in my excitement. But you'll be thorough, I know. But my gut reaction is telling me there is new data out there to be found. Now go home and prepare, and come the day after, go and seek out this evidence."

The following day passed more quickly than Bob thought it would. He was afraid the family was going to be quite disappointed in not going to Froth and with the new expedition set for only five days of activity instead of what was previously planned. But over all everyone agreed the trip to Mylako would be an exciting one, too, provided what the professor said could be true. Only Bob's son, Roger put up any resistance to the idea.

"I'm kind of glad and relieved we're not going to Froth," Nance said as she poured coffee. "I know you had your heart set on it, Bob. But with the children going, I feel much safer on Mylako. Besides, I really enjoyed our visit there years ago. Remember that lovely cottage where we stayed?"

"Yes, I remember. You were pregnant with Roger."

"Aw, mom!" Roger moaned. "I told all my friends we were going to the eastern area. They all thought it was neat. Everyone goes to Mylako."

"Not quite, son." Bob said while reaching for another piece of cake. "Many people have gone over the last several years, but only one in ten get their visa validated. The Mylakoans don't mind tourists, but they don't want their islands flooded with them. It seems to me when they got that law passed, a really wise decision was made."

"Your father is right, children." Nance chimed in. "When we were there, there was a certain charm to the place. Look what has happened to the northern area of Blackroth. A few years ago it became a hot tourist area, and now those small villages are tourist traps, and they are void of the joy and personality that once marked their existence. Besides, look at it this way, we'll have another week left of vacation time when we get back to do whatever you two children would like."

"Well, I'm glad just to be going," Sally said. "Besides, Roger, how many of your classmates and friends have been to the islands? After all, this will be the first trip you and I even took there."

"You think it's a big deal when we go ten miles to Wellington, so what do you know?" Roger countered.

"Enough, let's not get into your little arguments," Bob exclaimed. "Both of you go pack your clothes. You may wear canvas sneakers, but pack your hiking boots."

"And remember, just your clothes. You'll have enough to do," replied Nance. "We are going to help and learn with your father, so it's not just a fun trip."

"Come on, Nance," Bob said. "Don't make it sound like a chore. Kids, this is a safari into the heartland where even the natives no longer go. But remember, we are on a tight schedule."

"Alllriiight!" yelled Roger as he ran to his room.

"It won't be dangerous, will it Bob?" Nance said with sudden concern. "Is it true what you just said? I mean I thought the whole island was accessible now."

"Oh, the outer coastlines are your average living lands. But the forest of Mylako makes travel quite difficult due to its density. Only the most hardy islanders ever go into the depths of the forest, and that is for the hardwood needed for their carvings."

"Oh dear," Nance put her hand on her chin.

"Not to worry, honey. It's just that the forest is so thickly wooded that life in it is too harsh. There have been no reports of anything dangerous. That is except for the bears."

"The bears!" Nance yelped. "What bears? You never told me about bears on Mylako. No way are we subjecting ours lives to such danger."

"The expression on your face is priceless," laughed Bob.

Seeing that she had been fooled about the bears, she too started to giggle. "Sometimes you can be a scoundrel."

The rest of the evening was spent packing and of mild conversation. The family worked well as a unit for this was not their first excursion. There had been several others over the past three years. When Sally became eight and could handle some chores and assignments that her father gave her, then the whole family went together. Bob Troyer wanted each assignment to be an adventure for everyone, and for each adventure a learning trip. But this one was going to be their longest and most detailed.

Everyone admitted they had a hard time sleeping. The excitement of the trip now made each toss and turn, and sleep had come grudgingly. Still, what was several hours seemed like a few minutes, and morning was upon them. Quickly, the family moved about the house doing the little things that the new morning called for, and soon they were ready to go. Because everything was packed to go the evening before, they were soon in a taxi riding to the air dock.

"Driver! Before you drop us off at the dock, loop over to the end where the restaurant is located. I don't know about the rest of you, but I'm starving." exclaimed Bob.

"I am too, daddy," Sally cried out. "I'm also a little chilly," pulling her jacket closer to her.

"You know I heard the government is thinking of allowing the citizens to have ownership of their own automobiles," Bob said as he ran his hand upon the upholstery of his seat.

"Really, dad?" cried Roger. "Do you think we could own an automobile like this one day?"

"I said the government was considering it," laughed Bob. "There are many pros and cons to the subject. Right now the trains and taxies we have do the job. Perhaps in the future such travel will be commonplace, but right now the automobile is restricted to the use of today's thinking and guidelines."

"Enough of this talk, let's go eat," Nance said. "I'm starved. Driver, drop our luggage off at the dock, pier two, they are awaiting us."

"Good idea, my dear woman," Bob countered. "By the time he gets back we should all be finished eating."

Soon, with gaiety everyone was climbing the dock's stairs to the airship, Freedom. It was the second time all were going on one; the first time was for a pleasure ride, and the joy of it gave excitement to each in anticipation of this ride.

"Everyone seems in fine spirits," cried professor Moriarity as he stepped out of the captain's cabin to greet everyone. "All is prepared, Bob. The only thing missing is me. But the old legs would only bog you down. Nance, how good it is to see you."

"Oh professor!" hugged Nance. "Can't you at least ride to the islands with us and return with the ship?"

"By God, Bob, I believe I could do that. I could be back by noon."

"Hooray!" yelled Roger. "You can give me more lessons on checks and stones. I've even beaten dad a couple times."

"Oh! So you've been practicing, my little rascal," laughed Mr. Moriarity.

"Nance's idea is a good one professor." Bob intervened. "We can all get clued in on what we're about to do, so no games today, Roger boy. Come everyone! Let's get our baggage stowed away and get comfortable. What does the captain say about the weather and the flight, professor?'

"We couldn't have picked a better morning, Bob. All is clear, and in about ninety minutes we should be landing at Edonin in Mylako. Let's go sit down and get situated. We are about to lift off."

"Dad!" cries Roger. "Can I go up front and ride with the captain? Pleeeasse!"

"Me too, daddy, me too," pleaded Sally.

With a shrug of his shoulders, Moriarity looked at Bob. "He is an old friend of mine. Come children, I'll introduce you to him, a pirate if there ever was one."

Wide eyed, Sally stopped, "Really, Mr. Moriarity?"

"Why the man has flown over the seas clear to the mines of the East and knows the cloudy skies of all Froth," professor Moriarity spoke in hushed tones spreading his arms out. "Come, come, I'll let you shake his hand. But no galloping around his cabin. Friend or no friend, he'll throw us all out."

"Really, professor," laughed Nance. "You'll give them nightmares."

"Yes, perhaps. But so enthralled are they to be up front that they will give us peace and quiet here," Bob said.

"I talked to the surveyor that drew up the sketches over Mylako. He wasn't sure, because of the height and suddenness of the flight, but he feels the area he saw contained a good size building. Can you imagine that, a building right in the denseness of the forest." And with that the professor unrolled the sketches.

"Take the rest of the day to rest, and in the morning I have someone to help you. His name is Kanta, a top-notch guide of these islands. Although, with my dealings with him, even he never mentioned a building in this quadrant nor anywhere else deep in the forest."

"I dare say, professor," Nance chimed in, "Those islanders hardly ever talk about what they see or know about their homeland. I will admit though, a more gentle race does not exist anywhere."

"Won't the trip into the forest prove too much from Edonin?" Bob said, pointing to the map.

"Yes, if you go from the port's eastern limits. But Kanta will take you by boat north to a little town, more like a village, about seven kilometers from that quadrant, and from there you will safari about two or three kilometers inward and make camp. The following day you can proceed to that area. And believe me, Bob, I've been on that island time and again. To walk through that forest will be time consuming and taxing on everyone's nerves. Were it not your children going with you, I would say this trip would be too great for them. Even now I have some reservations."

"Oh dear! Will the children be safe?" Nance questioned with a worried tone.

"Oh quite safe. Kanta is a wonderful man. And if they listen to him, he will have them too busy to be bored or rowdy. Travel will just be exceedingly slow but not impossible." the professor replied.

"In all your travels there professor, why didn't you ever see some creation like this supposedly good size building?" asked Bob.

"Wait a minute, Bob," Moriarity interrupted. "You, yourself, have gone with me a couple trips along the shores and into the forest. Good grief, man, the trees and bush could hide this airship one hundred meters from us as we walked by it."

"No offense, professor," whispered Bob as he put his hand on the good man's back. "It just seems that of all the people I have known, you probably covered as much ground as anyone on the islands."

"Bob even told me you took trips on your own time and expense," Nance joined in.

"Yes, quite right the both of you." Moriarity replied. "And sometimes I would find nothing, absolutely nothing. But then when I went north and northeast, on a couple occasions I came across a few things that perplexed me. I told no one of course. Besides, everyone knows of my infatuation with the islands and the folklore involved. So rather than mention something about what could be nothing, I just kept quiet. And now this freak happenstance ties into some of the things I saw."

Perplexed, Bob cried out, "What! You never even told me about any find. What did you find?"

"Well, at three locations I discovered on the forest floor areas where the ground cover was thinner was something like a tough grass growing there. I mean no bushes or shrubs. At first I paid no attention until in the same area I saw two spots almost like links about three to four meters longs and just a meter or so across. I was about fifteen meters from them that the oddity of it made me stop."

"Was it a find of artifacts?" Nance cut in.

"No. There were no such findings. But I crawled around on my hands and knees there and discovered a pattern to it. It was exceedingly hard, thus explaining the no growth of heavy plant life."

The professor lit his pipe and hesitated. After a couple of puffs, he continued. "I came to the conclusion that what I found was a remnant of an ancient path or road. These links were about two meters wide, and this type of discovery was found a couple other places. After I studied the sketches from the Questor, what do you think I found?"

"Well, I certainly have no idea." Nance said.

"Let me guess, professor. They all pointed to the area on quadrant 117." Bob yelled out excitedly.

"Precisely!" Moriarity said clapping his hands together. "Find what is there and we may have the riddle at least to the path I found. You know, I am still in wonder over that find. How many years have passed only the spirits know, and yet portions of that road, I feel that is what it is, still is compacted enough to exist."

The rest of the trip passed quickly as the professor and Bob went over the check list of items brought on board, and of the sequence of events that was to be followed unless providence, for ill or good, intervened. Soon the outline of Mylako was visible, and the buildings of Edonin became clearer as the fine airship, Freedom, turned about to maneuver into the docking procedure. It caused a rush of excitement and exhilaration to everyone, and they all gathered on the western side to better see that ancient town from above, and to watch the captain delicately lower the landing apparatus.

From the lowering maneuver to docking, it took only five minutes so smoothly did the landing go. And the unloading of all luggage was done quickly by porters who appeared seemingly out of nowhere. Soon the Troyers were loading everything on board the carriage that was to take them to the inn where they were to spend the night.

"Oh! I wish we had more of these back home, daddy" Sally squealed with delight as she climbed up the step into the carriage. "Will two horses be able to pull us all?"

"Don't you worry, missy," the tall driver called out. "Why they could carry twice the load you are putting on this old buggy. Is this your first ride on a horse carriage?"

"Yes it is, and I do think it is such a lovely buggy. But won't you get wet if it rains?" Sally observed, seeing that the driver would be sitting up front and outside.

"Well, we try not to," he laughed. "I keep a raincoat and boots under my seat. Even got a hookup for an umbrella. Protects me from the sun more than the rain."

He lifted the last item up on the rack. "What about you, young man, this your first ride, too?"

"Oh, no sir," Roger exclaimed. "There are a few horse drawn carriages back home. I mean not right where we live, but on the continent, especially up north. My dad is an anthropologist and sometimes we get to travel with him, just like on this trip."

After settling down, Roger spoke again. "By the way, mister, why aren't there any motor cars on the islands?"

"It's just the way of life here, son. Besides, it allows our islands to stay more peaceful. Whoever made the decision made a wise one, I think. Besides, I understand those things stink up the air."

"He is right, you know," laughed Bob. "Maybe our government should only let the transit companies and the military use motorcars. Maybe too many of them would cause a polluted atmosphere."

The trip to the inn proved as pleasant as the flight. As they entered the main street, the sound of the horse hooves on the cobblestones proved to be a relaxing sound that had each rider gently swaying to its steady beat.

The inn appeared like a very large house, but once inside, the spaciousness of the rooms surprised everyone. The dining area had a warm glow about it and an elegance that reminded both Bob and Nance of the social club they belonged to at the university. After unpacking what they needed for the night's stay, they went to the dining area for dinner. It was late afternoon, but such an early start on the evening meal was agreed upon for the trip made everyone hungry, and hopefully an early bedtime would find all rested for a full day's activity.

Only a few people came and went while the Troyers leisurely ate a drawn out meal consisting of five courses of the native cooking.

"My goodness," Bob sighed. "That was one fine meal. Would you believe we have been here almost two hours? Children go to your room and get ready for bed. Your mother and I are going to have one more cup of coffee. Oh waiter!" he called out to the elderly man who had been serving them.

The children pushed their chairs in and walked towards the doorway. Both appeared glad to leave after sitting for so long. And the elderly man was pouring a rich dark coffee into the waiting cups.

"That was a fabulous dinner," Nance uttered. "But I noticed not too many people came here to eat. How can you stay open, if you will excuse my abruptness."

"Thank you for the compliment, madam," the waiter answered. "Today being Thursday, it is our slowest day. As for staying open and in business," he somewhat chuckled to himself, "why this inn has been owned and run by my family for over four hundred years. The upkeep does not take much, just to meet the taxes, mainly. And the tourist trade we get easily meets that demand, and the islanders eat here often enough to provide a comfortable living. By the way, excuse my abruptness, and to satisfy my curiosity, but by the size of the luggage dropped off here, you'll be staying here longer than most tourists are allowed. May I ask what you'll be doing here?"

"Not at all, my good man," replied Bob. "I'm an anthropologist, and my family and I will head north tomorrow to do some searching into the forest. We have only a few days to do it, but we have a very good idea where we are going. By chance, do you know my good colleague and dear friend, professor Moriarity?"

15

"What a wonderful fellow," gleefully resounded the old man. "Many a time the professor has stayed here, many a time we have talked well into the night. Why you must be Bob Troyer, and this must be Nancy."

Extending his hand, Bob spoke. "Yes, I am; and this is my wife. You must have a good memory, but her name is Nance."

"Tell me, why isn't the professor here? I do have something I have wanted to show him. What is up north that you wish to see?"

"Well, to make a quick story, a surveyor from the airship, Questor, which was blown off course during the last storm, drew a sketch that showed a building in the area we labeled quadrant seventeen. In all the professor's safaris on the island, he never came across any ancient structures. You know the professor, he is going crazy with excitement, but his legs won't allow him physically any kind of long treks. I don't expect to find anything, but one never knows; besides, it will be a fun trip for all of us."

The old man glanced around the room, not so much in secret but so as not to break the social etiquette in his role of waiter. Quietly he spoke, "Do you mind if I sit for a moment?"

"No, of course not!" Nance and Bob repeated.

"The professor and I became fast friends over the many years and visits. Many of his colleagues feel he puts too much desire for hunting old stories about the islands. But this is precisely what cements our friendship. By the way, forgive my rudeness, my name is Levi Lukins. My wife Mary and me own this old inn. Soon, my son Jackson, who does the cooking most of the time with his mother's help, will inherit this place."

"Does this inn have a name?" Nance asked.

"Yes, it is the Asher Inn. The sign got blown from its post during that last storm you mentioned."

"Before we go any further, if your name is Lukins, why is this the Asher Inn?" Bob asked.

"Truthfully, I don't know. But when I was a boy my father ran this inn and would tell wonderful stories about this place, stories he heard form his father. Not many people know this, but according to my father, this was once called the King's Inn."

"You mean then it was changed to the name, Asher Inn?" Bob asked as he took a sip from his cup filled with a deep aromatic coffee.

"Oh no!" Lukins replied. "I mean the kings of these islands slept here and ate here. This was considered like a second home to the royalty of the islands."

"It does have an elegant and regal bearing to it." Nance spoke. "But I don't remember hearing about it when the two of us were here last."

"Like I said, very few know of its history. To them it's just another inn, and to be here or to the other two mean nothing to most people."

"Imagine," Bob almost whispered. "Kings that we don't even know about in days long ago, so long ago we don't have records of. Not even Moriarity mentioned this."

"I told Mr.Moriarity, and you know now. But no one else except family knows. You are here for knowledge, others would be here for exploitation."

The wonder of such things happening long ago still hung over Bob like a cloud of rosemoor smoke, which lifted the spirits while dulling the body movements. It was a few seconds more before he sensed his trance like state, and quickly he focused his attention back to the present. Nance smiled, knowing that such thoughts came along so infrequently, but that such encounters were the reason Bob so enjoyed his work. Levi sensed it too, so he sat calmly in the silence of the moment.

"What was it you were going to show the professor?" queried Bob. "I would be honored to hear your knowledge."

"I found an old map in the wine cellar about a year ago, but I was not going to trust it to that dang mail service we have to ship it to the professor. Should it have gotten lost anyone else would have thrown it away. Besides, it is part of this place. Anyhow, I must admit it slipped my mind, and seeing you here brings it back to me."

"I will be glad to give it to the professor on the return trip home. And he will see to it that it is shipped directly back to you when he is finished with it, Mr. Lukins."

"Please, address me as Levi, for a friend of the professor is my friend. Besides, he talked of you often, like you was his son. He is very proud of you."

He poured more coffee and continued. "I won't keep you too long. The map I have I'll show you in the morning. It shows where an old castle stood."

"A castle here on the islands! Really, Mr. Lukins, I mean Levi, I've been here before, in fact, part of our honeymoon was spent here, and as we visited, never did a castle or its existence come in to our knowledge. As I said earlier, even professor Moriarity never mentioned it." Bob said in loud voice that caused a few heads to turn in their direction.

"Ah! My dear fellow! This may be a sideline for you to develop a history of the islands. But for the professor, well, this is his love, his driving force. He knew that a kingdom existed here. He even felt that such a kingdom should have left more than just small artifacts and other such tidbits to be found. But he had no proof. Now with this map, and I do say it is an old, old thing, but quite well preserved, he can formulate his thesis with greater conviction. And I do say I'm very happy to help him."

"Bob! The children are waiting for us. We will be having breakfast here, Mr. Lukins. Could you bring the map then?" Nance intervened.

"She is quite right; and the children are waiting. But do tell me, is the castle nearby?" Bob countered. Nance grimaced at what she thought

18

might be a longer delay, but Bob held one finger up to her while he looked straight at Lukins.

"I'll have the map here right along with breakfast." Mr. Lukins replied. "It really should be a surprise to the professor; in fact, to most anybody because the castle is less than four kilometers to the west, inland about a half kilometer. I've walked that area as soon as I could after discovering the map. Without knowing it, one can easily go past it, but knowing what to look for allowed me to focus on the area more fully. Oh it's there all right. Imagine! Right under our noses all these decades."

"Surely not in its entirety?" Bob questioned.

"Oh, heavens no. But the base is there. It's covered quite well by plant growth. There seems to be a labyrinth to the layout. In fact, I found what looks to be a stairway and a heavy doorway. It was well hidden, and only by luck did I see it. But then I was too tired, and I am too old to have been able to force it open. When you get back from your expedition I'll take you there." Mr. Lukins responded with excitement.

"To tell you the truth," Lukins continued, "I've been wanting to know what was down there. But I don't trust anyone to go there. Oh my! I'm rambling on."

He stepped by Nance's chair and pulled it out for her. "Please try the poached eggs and sausage. It's a hearty meal with Mrs. Lukins' biscuits. And the sausage is from an old recipe. You should find it most delightful." And he started to chuckle to himself.

"May I ask what is so funny, Mr. Lukins?" Nance smiled as she asked.

"Oh nothing. Excuse my rudeness. It's just that lately everything seems to be old. Old Levi, old recipe, old castle, old inn." And with that statement he seemed to chuckle louder.

As they lay in bed, Bob stared up at the ceiling. Nance watched him for a while before she reached over to tap his nose. "What's the matter, darling?"

Jerking somewhat as from a trance, Bob turned his face towards her. "I just keep thinking about that map, and Mr. Lukins, and his story. I expected to spend a few days here looking over an area that probably won't produce anything. Truthfully, this trip was to be a combination vacation and appeasement."

"Appeasement! What do you mean?"

"I was coming here just to please the professor. He seemed so excited when he saw those sketches. Now I see why he didn't tell me about the inn, and Mr. Lukins, and other things about this place. I may be no better than the other fine colleagues who ridicule that fine man behind his back. Lukins was right. I was just skimming the top of this place's history, while for the professor it's his love."

"Don't be so hard on yourself, honey," Nance softly replied. "You've done some fine work for the professor on these islands. I've never known you to be lacking in any of your projects. You've never given anything but your best. Besides, you've been more analytical, while the professor has always showed more emotion concerning these islands."

"That's just what I've been thinking. He always said your heart can sometimes be your best guide. It allows you to see things that aren't there and to feel things you can't see. I lack that insight because sometimes I'm too analytical. But thanks, dear," Bob said as he reached over to kiss his wife. "But now there seems to be more than meets the eye. We'll find out soon enough. We better get a good night's sleep. Good night, honey."

"Good night, dear." Nance replied as she reached over to put out the flickering light. She felt Bob's hand reach over to hold hers, and then a numbness swept over her.

It had been an exciting day after all for everyone thought Bob. The flight was enjoyable as it always seemed to be, and the story Mr. Lukins told him caused an excitement in him that now wore him out. It had been several minutes since saying goodnight, and he could hear the children sleeping deeply as opposed to last night, and now sleep was finally bringing its shroud over him. He willingly closed his eyes and let its gentleness overcome him.

A knocking on the door awakened Bob, and a voice calling out that it was a wake up call. Nance rolled over and let out a soft moan of contentment as she snuggled deeper into the feather filled pillow. But as he walked across the floor, he heard the children awake and talking in the next room.

"Anybody in there hungry?" he blurted out.

"I am!" cried Roger.

"Me too!" echoed Sally.

"Me three," Bob said as he splashed water from the basin onto his face. "Let's get dressed. We have a great breakfast awaiting us and one long day."

The three of them quickly dressed, and Bob had to shake Nance to again tell her to wake up. She groaned and then stretched. "Oh! This bed feels so heavenly," as she swung herself into a sitting position.

"I'll go with Roger and Sally to secure our baggage for our trip. You clean up and pack this stuff in the small suitcase. We'll be back soon ready to eat, so prepare yourself." He then gave her a slap on the backside, and then he leaned over to kiss her forehead.

"Come on, kids, time to earn your keep."

"Yes sir!" Roger responded with a snappy salute and a mock clicking of his heels together.

"Oh, daddy," Sally gleefully cried. "I think this will be so much fun." And she hurried out the door with them.

Nance washed herself, dressed, and was finishing packing when the door swung open by the returning family. Within minutes all four were entering the dining area. It was empty except for a portly gentleman sitting across the room reading a paper and drinking coffee. They sat down at a table next to a great window that allowed them to look into the town.

They could see out upon the cobblestone street into the very heart of the town. A few lights shone from some of the homes and a couple of stores, but the only activity to be seen was the horse drawn cab slowly coming towards them from out of the slight mist which enveloped the area. But the day was warming rapidly and the sky was clear.

"It's so peaceful looking, isn't it?" whispered Nance. "Why we never visited this inn before, I'll never know."

"Probably the most beautiful part of the day by Mrs. Lukins standards," Levi Lukins spoke as he turned the cups right side up and poured hot coffee into them. Immediately the aroma filled the air, and Nance inhaled deeply as she smiled up at the man. "Myself, I like the midday. By then the day has settled itself and knows where it stands for the most part. Is everybody hungry?"

"Starving!" Cried out Sally.

"Me too!" echoed Roger.

Levi laughed. "I've ordered for everyone. I hope no one minds the liberty I took in doing so. Not to try Mrs. Lukins specialty would be a culinary mistake on your part and a poor guide on my part."

"I do believe you've sold us, Mr.Lukins, I mean Levi," Nance said. "Mmmmm, the coffee smells great. I would like a tall glass of milk for each of the children if you have it please."

"Coming right up. And for a real treat for our special guests, Mrs. Lukins got up a tad earlier and prepared her world famous walnut butter rolls to top off the meal, a delight that would have truly pleased the kings that dined here." And with that he walked back towards the kitchen area.

"I can't help but feel drawn towards him. I feel as though we've been friends and have dined here often. And yet, we've never been here in our last two visits. Still, a warm person whom I'm sure does not treat everyone like he does us," spoke Bob.

"Kings! What kings?" Roger asked. "Were there really kings here, dad?"

"Only in stories that we've heard in a time long, long ago," Bob replied. "However, professor Moriarity really believes the stories to be true. Our excursion here might shed some light on the matter. Mr. Lukins even talked of a map last night. Although, it won't surprise me if it is a simple collection of scribbling and nothing exact."

"You certainly felt differently last night; in fact, I doubt if you went to bed right away just thinking about it," Nance uttered.

"This is going to be great, daddy," Sally squealed. "Will we see a castle or anything like that?"

"Honey, we will be lucky to find some old stones," Nance answered back. "Maybe when we get back, Mr Lukins can show us the so called castle he found."

She no longer spoke those words when Lukins arrived with a tray heaped with plates emitting steaming and delicious aromas. He quickly and proficiently served each person before he spoke. "After breakfast, my friend, I'll show the map I talked about last night. In the meantime, eat. The sausage is good anytime but superb when it's hot." And with that he quickly left and ambled over to the only other diner to check on his condition.

"Oh my, this is good!" Bob said as he took a sip of coffee following a mouthful of the food.

"You better believe it," Nance chimed in, and all nodded their approval.

Very little was said as the meal was quickly consumed. And no sooner was everyone done that Mr. Lukins arrived with a pot of coffee, and trailing him was a short handsome woman carrying a covered platter. Lukins quickly gathered up the plates and replaced them with smaller ones.

"Mr. and Mrs. Troyer, I want you to meet my wife, Mary."

She smiled and curtsied before setting the platter in the middle of the table. Lifting the cover revealed a round puffy pastry, glazed and covered with walnuts, hot with butter melting down the sides. The warm baked aroma filled the table area quickly, and in a chorus, the Troyers sniffed and let out ahs.

"How nice it is to meet you, Mrs. Lukins," Bob replied as he stood up to meet her. "Levi was understating your meal when he said it was very good. It was fabulous."

"I thought I was stuffed until I smelled this pastry," Nance said as she extended her hand in greetings.

"It is my pleasure to meet you folks, also," replied Mary. "Levi and I are especially happy to meet Mr. Moriarity's good friends. We use to have many happy hours together, and he talked of you as his family, and especially of you, Mr. Troyer, you are his son. Said he was a mite hard on you at times, but also felt you could handle it. You are a crown in his book. He is also one very good storyteller. Tell him we miss him and to come back here soon."

"Well, I ... I'm flattered, Mrs Lukins," stammered Bob. "But he never dwells on this place in our conversations. It is such a lovely place, too."

"Yes!" followed Nance. "He would babble on for hours about Mylako and the other islands. I am charmed to be here but dismayed at his leaving this inn and you people out of his conversations. Any reason as to why he would choose to do that?"

Levi smiled and took Mary by the arm and turned to go. "Eat your pastry while it's hot. I'll be back."

Nance looked at Bob and he just shrugged his shoulders. Quickly, they devoured the pastry and helped themselves to another cup of coffee. Bob asked the children to go outside to check on things that they eagerly complied. As they departed, Levi approached the table with a scroll under his arm.

"My good people, I didn't mean to leave your question hanging in the air like that, but as you found out, Mrs. Lukins' rolls are delightful when fresh and hot. Allow me to join you two."

Pushing the dishes to a side, he unrolled the scroll. "I don't think this is a form of paper but a light skin. It certainly is durable, and as you see, quite legible," he offered.

"My good Mrs. Troyer," he continued. "We people of the islands are proud and a close knit group. To get to know us well is very uncommon. But your professor has become one of us, accepted in every way freely. Did he ever confide in you that his grandmother was born here?"

Before either could speak, he motioned them to silence. "That is a matter that you should discuss with him. In fact, I may have exceeded my boundaries on that statement. Nonetheless, our islands and its unknown legacy are his driving passion. We know this and respect it fully. In turn, we offer him our open friendship and will help him in anyway. There are a great many of us that would like to know our heritage, too. Look upon the map and see for yourself. Why, there must have been a royal family and nobility that ruled us years ago. To own and run this inn still excites and pleases me and my family as it has my father and his before him."

"Why this is priceless!" exclaimed Bob. His hand delicately touched the edges of the map. Its figures and symbols shown clearly, and he drew it closer to him.

"You say you have seen this castle, I mean its remains?" Bob inquired.

"Yes," Levi answered. "It's not far from here. The outer edge of the forest is regaining its hold on it. But the foundation is still visible to the trained eye, especially when you know what to look for."

"And you say you know of a stairwell down into the foundation?" Bob inquired as he still delicately rubbed the edges of the map.

"Yes," Levi replied. "Its covered by brush and broken bits of masonry. From one side of the area it's almost completely invisible, but approached from the other side when the sun hits its side, an outline is defined, and when looked upon, a descending structure. I must say, I was over that spot several times and was fortunate to be at the right spot when the sun hit it."

"And not even the professor knows of it?" Nance joined in with excitement in her voice. "His excitement will be overwhelming when he hears of it. Although, with what we have seen the last few hours, I mean … this place, you, the map … I am surprised Bob didn't know more of the professor's excursions in to the land."

"As I mentioned before, the professor thought much of you, Mr. Troyer," Lukins spoke softly. "But he knew you were really concerned with the eastern area of Victoriana and the deep parts of Froth. It has been an issue that has taken your interest the past three or four years if I am correct."

Bob nodded and was about to speak, but Lukins continued. "He considers you the finest researcher in the country, Mr. Troyer. So the professor wanted to gain as much information to present to you as he could so his passion would also appear to have a convincing background. Besides, he also feels that the land of Froth and these islands have an interlocking history. Imagine how shocking it would be to the establishment to think that such places may have had a more appealing, or as I would like to think, a more adventurous history. No, my son, he wanted more data for even you, but also your work would become a supplement to back up his research."

"I suppose you are correct," Bob answered as he looked to Nance. "I have been at times preoccupied with my research. I even have to admit I felt mine was more valuable than his. I was going to use extensive use of the airship we have available and now here is this map. If it is truly authentic, and no slight to you, Mr. Lukins, this will be just as important. I can honestly say I am looking forward to this trip. My only regret will be the brevity of it. We have been given only one week from the university to check out this discovery of the building. Had we known about the map, perhaps the professor could have received more funds and time."

"And I can honestly say I am too, darling," Nance spoke as she clasped his hand and drew forth to kiss him.

"Well! Enough said," Lukins cried out smiling. "Your guide, Kanta, should be waiting for you outside. If I know him, and I do, he should be entertaining the children with some slight of hand tricks. Here, take this map lest we forget it, and keep it with you to give to the professor on the return trip. It will give you time to study it over the next few days too."

"Is this man, Kanta, a good guide, Mr. Lukins, I mean Levi?" Nance asked as she took his arm as they walked towards the door.

"The best, Mrs. Troyer. He will go deep into the woods for days on end. Usually on his return he is quiet and solemn for a while. He calls it his cleansing trips. You may have a hard journey, but he'll always bring you back."

Parked next to the main door of the inn was the same carriage that brought them there the previous evening. The children stood in front of the horses, while a tall man was moving his arms about the horses' heads, and the children's gleeful laughter could be heard.

Sally saw her parents and walked towards them. "Oh, mom! Mr. Kanta seems to pull objects from everywhere, and even now is pulling them from the horses' ears. It is so funny. I know it's a trick, but I can't see how he does it."

The tall man stopped his act when he saw the Troyers and approached them. He was thin but muscular and graceful in manner. His face was illuminated with a flowing mustache and eyes that gleamed, but a scar curved from his left ear across his cheekbone down to his lip. Only his flashing smile prevented him from having a sinister bearing. He spoke with a soft yet deep voice. "I am Kanta," giving a slight bow before them. "Professor Moriarity has sent word of your coming, and he asked me to watch over you. By his request, I respectfully become your guide."

"Levi said you like children and like to do magic," Nance spoke first. "Apparently, you've won over the children. It seems to me a strange combination ... magician and adventurer. Levi tells us you search and know these islands better than anyone." Almost curtly, she added, "Tell me, Kanta, how do you rate yourself?"

Bowing low, Kanta replied, "I am a first rate guide, but an amateur magician, madam." Gazing into her eyes and speaking low, he questioned, "Does the lady feel insecure with Kanta, or does the expedition worry her?"

Sensing that in his reply, he felt her sudden uneasiness, and she answered. "Please forgive my brashness, Mr. Kanta, if I may call you that, but I always feel nervous starting any of Bob's trips, especially with the children with us. Perhaps as we travel you can tell me why there isn't much exploring of these islands' interiors by the very people who live here. Besides being lost, there have been no reports of anything that can harm anyone; and yet, the forest of Mylako is almost unknown even by your islanders. What's the big secret or why the apathy? Oh dear, I'm afraid my nerves just got the best of me knowing we are really starting."

"Maybe Kanta will answer, my dear," Bob spoke. "But let's all get going towards the pier while the day is young. Come children! Climb aboard and make way for a great day."

The horses' hooves sang out on the cobblestone with a pleasant melody, and the quaintness of the town was soothing to the eye. Each one seized their own view and spoke nothing, absorbing the joy of the morning and the sight of the land. And soon the pier was before them.

Bob looked over to Nance and gave her a reassuring smile. "I'm just fine now, Bob. Once this carriage started moving, the worry was swept along with it."

Within minutes, the clamoring of baggage being unloaded, then reloaded, was done, and the farewell was said to the coachman. The sails were popped open, and the boat easily skimmed across the water riding a parallel course to the shore heading north to the village of Andson.

"Tell me, Kanta," Bob spoke. "Has anything changed much over the last few years? We were there on our honeymoon, and it was a lovely place."

"Andson seems never to change, sir," Kanta answered. "Very few mainlanders go there, and tradition is very strong there and over the whole island entity. We like things as they are."

"Why the name Andson?" asked Sally. "Was it named after something or someone in particular?"

"The professor said it was named after someone, as most places are, honey," Bob answered her. "But he nor anyone else knows who or what it was named after. Our records don't go back that far. It's a strange world we live in. We know much has happened years ago, but it seems as though a great calamity has removed from us any telltale signs. I feel that some answers lie in the area of Froth, and the professor feels the answers may be in these islands."

Looking out into the sea, Kanta replied. "You both may be right, Mr. Troyer, you both may be right."

The children scurried back and forth across the boat. The hull was greatly curved which gave it an ungainly appearance, and it moved slowly but relentlessly towards its goal. The flat surface from side to side gave it room for much cargo, and the hull beneath provided a roomy dry interior by which a comfortable ride could be given during storms and rains.

There weren't many of these boats because many were not needed. The cargo shipped from island port to island port was sufficient enough in quantity to keep the island supplied, whether it was foodstuff or other goods. The captains of these vessels traveled from island to island and occasionally to the continent using only a skill acquired by generations of piloting to guide them. In fact, the crews consisted of family units that used the boats as their homes as well as business enterprises. It was by these boats that news was spread from island to island.

Only government issued trips from islands to the mainland were allowed. Though capable of such travel, these trips were fewer made. This way was slow and tricky if not treacherous. Now the modern airships accounted for most travel and shipping. But even these modern inventions somehow could not replace the majesty of these seemingly ancient vessels. Slow, yes, but one felt part of the sea as well as the ship as it glided ever so sure to its destination.

"What are you thinking about, Kanta?" asked Nance, as she walked up to the rail where he stood. "I cannot help but feel joyful riding in one of these boats."

"Yes, Mrs. Only two things give me gladness. The forest is one and to travel on the sea is the second."

"Mr. Lukins said something I thought was unusual when we were at the inn. He said you felt cleansed by your trips into the forest. Why?" she probed.

"It is a place from whence came my ancestors. I know of the woods as no man, even the islanders. I feel as though their spirits live there."

Kanta spoke softly, his deep voice easily overpowering the sound of the waves slapping the boat's sides.

"I would think that would be frightening," Nance replied.

"At first, yes. It was almost terrifying."

"And now, what do you feel now?"

He turned towards her, leaning against the rail and looking at her but with a far away stare. Seconds passed before he spoke. "Awe! I feel awe in the forest. After my initial fright, I realized it was the chill of the shade and the wind whispering through the trees that startled me when I ventured deep into the forest. I was a very young man then, not much older than your son. I was always going into the woods. It seemed to draw me as a magnet draws iron, but that one day I traveled deeper than ever before when the fear came to me and I felt lost and so terribly alone. I sat down and cried, cried until I fell asleep. When I awoke, everything seemed so peaceful, and I just sat and looked over the beauty of the forest. When I started walking, it was as though someone kind was guiding me. Soon reason overcame emotion, and I left to go home never afraid again."

"Did you tell anyone else of this experience?"

"I had a few playmates that really cared about the forest. The ones I played with would venture into the forest's edge, but only I would go deep into its interior. Surprisingly, my best friend was an old man from whom I continuously sought guidance. He taught me much, and I did tell him of that trip. He did not say much when I told him except that I may have been blessed. I'm afraid I've talked too much already."

Bob appeared from the hold carrying two cups of hot liquid in his left hand and a one cup in his right. "Here, have some delicious soup made by the captain's wife. This boat holds everything one would need to live quite comfortably. What have you two been talking about while I've been below?"

"Let's just say its Kanta's growing up ritual into the guide he is today," Nance spoke as she clasped both hands around the cup. "Do you know where we are wanting to go, Kanta?"

"Yes, Kanta!" Bob echoed. "Mr. Moriarity received a map which showed an opening with a square in it. Do you know what he could mean by it?"

"Ah, yes, that which I call the cottage in the woods."

"Cottage!" Bob cried out, almost choking on the soup he started to sip. "Do you mean there is a building in the forest. Surely it's just some woodsman's shack."

"No!" Kanta answered. "This building is large. Several rooms big. It was well built for it stands in one piece. The wood it is made of is thick and strong. I walked around it several times. It is built well. But I have been there only once. Though I know the forest well, I came upon it by accident. For us to come upon it, we will have to again be very lucky."

"What does it look like inside?" Bob asked,

"I have not been inside. The door is blocked shut, and I do not wish to do any damage. I am at one with the forest and to do so would break this unity. But I do know one thing about it."

"It is very, very old."

Kanta walked to the rail across from them and just stared out to the sea. He didn't talk anymore, and Bob and Nance asked no further questions. They called the children over to go down below to eat.

Soon, the harbor appeared and the town of Andson loomed before them. The unpacking of their baggage was skillfully done so that in a few minutes it was finished. After thanking the crew, everyone walked along the pier to the street adjacent to it. As in Edonin, the streets were cobblestones and even less traffic was apparent.

"Know what, daddy?" Sally inquired.

Kanta answered before Bob could reply. "It is but noonday. We can go to an abandoned shed I use on the outskirts of town. There, we will repack our luggage into knapsacks for easier carrying. I also have the food we will need. No one will go hungry for our days in the woods. After a short rest Mr. Troyer, I suggest we move into the forest before evening. I know of a clearing big enough to pitch camp."

"I guess you are prepared," Bob spoke, "And you are right. To tell the truth, I am anxious to get to that cottage as soon as possible. Come on everybody, our safari has started."

The children cheered, and all marched to the shed where the supplies awaited them. The streets that fanned off from the main boulevard were narrow but uncluttered by neither traffic nor objects. It was the third one from the left pointing north that Kanta lead them down, and whenever someone was met or showed themself from a doorway, Kanta gave a nod of recognition which was received and returned. The shed stood near a midsize barn where the sound of a saw cutting wood was heard. No person revealed themself, so Kanta opened the shed door, stepped inside, and quickly handed out canvas bags and various camping items.

"The food will outweigh the other items," Kanta spoke. "If each of us carries what I have distributed, we can eat well for a few days in the forest. Tell me little ones! Do you think you are big enough to help Kanta?"

"Oh yes, Kanta!" Sally cried out excitedly.

"I know I can," Roger replied. "I've helped my dad before on other trips, right dad?"

Bob laughed. "Of course, son, even though they were picnics, we walked far and you did great."

Roger beamed, and he handed his mother a large bag. She struggled for a moment to adjust the weight and fix the straps. But soon she had it balanced on her back, and she was helping the children with theirs as Bob went through the same motions.

"Each one of you take one of these poles. They will seem heavy and unnecessary at first, but they will help you keep your balance and to walk easier," Kanta said as he handed each a pole that seemed to be cut in size for each member. "We will put some distance between this town and us. In this sack I have some very good sandwiches made by the Lukins, and as we get near the forest edge, we will eat."

No one spoke as they walked in a single file behind Kanta. Each one was too busy looking down in the trail, watching each step, and getting use to the cadence of the foot hitting the ground and thrust of the pole.

The ground sloped upward very slightly, and the trail was unimpeded by any brush or heavy growth. The breathing became heavier, but still no one complained. Kanta smiled to himself when no one asked for rest, knowing it was physically draining on those not use to such labor. He knew the children were struggling, and he marveled at this family as all of them marched onward. He pushed on waiting for the sound that never came.

It had been almost over a hour since they left Andson, and the forest's edge was now underneath their feet. Selecting a large log that was lying nearby, Kanta plopped down on it and motioned the Troyers over to it. He opened the sack he had carried and took out the sandwiches.

"Oh my goodness!" Nance replied. "It feels so good to stop. And the thought of one of those sandwiches made me hungrier and hungrier."

Kanta smiled and tousled the children's hair. "I am very proud of you little ones," he spoke, and then he handed each a sandwich. "I have led bigger people who were unable to follow me without complaining. You've done much walking before, have you?"

Bob took his sandwich and responded. "Yes! They have traveled a few miles with me on weekend walks in the country. My work calls for walking more than most sciences, and these two enjoy doing it. I, too, am proud of them."

"Have you taken many people into the forest, Kanta?" Nance asked. "With all these provisions, you seemed well prepared for travel as though you've done this often. I haven't heard of any islander being that informal with the mainlanders. I mean most visits here consist of village or town sightseeing."

Kanta pulled out a large skin bag and uncorked the end that was pointed. He squirted cold water from it into his mouth, and then he held it for Sally. She tilted her head back as he did and let the refreshing liquid gush in as she gulped it down. He then repeated the act upon Roger.

"Oh! That's good, Kanta," Sally exclaimed." It seems so much colder and sweeter than ours. Is the water like that everywhere here?"

"No, little one," Kanta replied with a grin. "But throughout the forest there are brooks that jump out of the ground and stream for a while, then they seem to flow back into it again. This is such water, clean, pure, and cold."

He passed the bag to Mrs. Troyer. She struggled somewhat with it before she had it balanced where she could force the water out into a slow steady stream. When she was done and passed it onto Bob, Kanta spoke. "What you say is true, Mrs. Troyer. We are respectful to all people, but we don't get too friendly with the tourist. To supplement my income, I guide some of them along the shoreline and up to the forest. I even do some magician tricks if children are along. What I do here for you, I do for Mr. Moriarity, and if you are half the man he said you are, Mr. Troyer, I do this gladly. Besides, it's good to be back in the woods again."

Everyone continued eating, and soon the meal was finished. The backpacks were reluctantly put back on, and the march once again proceeded. But the rest and food gave their steps more bounce, and Roger even started to whistle.

They entered the forest, and it was as though they were walking into another zone of existence. The trees were still sparsely scattered, but the undergrowth around them much thinner. It was only a few minutes of following Kanta before the forest entirely enveloped them.

Now the rays of sunshine were intermingled with darkness causing caricatures of shadows and shades of green. The trees now stood about them in tall straight majestic splendor, and though there was ample space between them, their number caused an illusion of an incredible mass, which by looking about gave a view of a solid wall of bark.

The forest floor was not crowded by heavy growth, but the blanket of an infinite amount of leaves formed a matted carpet that was several inches deep. The floor crackled with the dry leave topping, but more so from the snapping of unseen twigs that blanketed the area as the safari trampled onward. For several hundred meters it seemed as though there was no rhyme or reason to Kanta's lead, because no walkway that resembled a trail presented itself.

The passage continued at an even pace, and time seemed neither to stop nor move for it seemed not to exist, and no one spoke except to call attention to a sound heard or a sight to be seen. No one complained about the burden they carried, although each would stop momentarily to shift their weight to relieve the unaccustomed stress.

Suddenly, a gurgling sound was heard, and Kanta led them to it. "Soon we will rest for a few minutes," he spoke. And he followed the stream that seemed to have popped out of the ground, just as he said they did at the last rest stop. He followed its course for about two hundred meters where they came upon an opening, and this is where he stopped. He dropped his large bag and swung his pack off his shoulders. Everyone gladly followed suit.

"Whew!" Nance sighed. "I must admit I started getting tired back there. And you poor children must be exhausted, too. How long have we been walking, Kanta?"

"Close to a hour and a half," he replied.

"How can you tell surrounded by all these trees?" Roger asked.

Kanta laughed and then replied. "I have been into the forest many times. After a while, the angle of the sun's rays as they filter through the trees give a good indication of time."

He bent over his pack and pulled from it a fluffy towel and handed it to Sally. "Take this and dip it into the water, then rub it on your face and arms. You'll feel like a newly rested person. Everyone take turns to refresh yourselves," he spoke.

He also pulled out a large ladle and handed it to Nance. She did not have to be told what to do but was instantly dipping it into the stream. The sweet water was consumed by large gulps, and everyone repeated her act, just as they did with the cold wet towel.

Bob sat next to Kanta while everyone found a spot to sit and rest. "Did you ever tell professor Moriarity about the cottage?"

"No!" Kanta replied. "I live south most of my life, and it was only a couple years ago when I moved into Andson. The cottage lies in the northerly direction of the island. The forest is very big, Mr. Troyer, and it would be quite easy to miss many things."

"The professor discovered some paths in the forest when he was here the last time, Kanta" Bob countered. "In fact, he found more than one path, and they all seem to point to that cottage. Why do you suppose that is so?"

Kanta hesitated for several moments before he spoke. "My people have lived here for as long as we know. But our history is not clear to us so I don't want to say what might not be so. However, I do know that cottage is not just some woodsman's hut. It is large and well built. In fact, it is in excellent condition. It had to be used by many, and if I miss my guess, by a royal family."

"A royal family?" Sally shouted. "Oh, Kanta! Do you think kings and queens lived there? How exciting."

"And probably a very pretty princess who looked just like you," Kanta replied. And he picked up his pack and started to put it on. "I want to go about five more kilometers deeper into the forest where we will camp for the night. That will put us very close to the cottage so early morning we can be there. But I must add, these next few kilometers will be very taxing."

Soon they were on their way, and the packs suddenly felt much heavier than before the break. Soon too, the breathing became more labored and sweat flowed freely from everyone. And because the campsite was a good distance from where they just rested, time now seemed to stand still.

The sunlight flowed through the treetops, but now filtered down more widely than before, and the shadows grew deeper and looked even more eerie.

How beautiful and how magnificent this forest is, thought Bob as he continuously gazed up and about the trees. Without the others here, this could even be a foreboding place with its dancing shadows and endless ocean of bark and leaves. But his thoughts kept bouncing back to Levi's map and castle then to the cottage where they were now trudging. Why was this island's history so unknown? By all accounts, its people were here as long as the people of the mainland. What seemed to have washed away their heritage. Ah! But these beautiful trees.

It seemed strange to him that everything that was going on was involving him and not his friend and colleague, professor Moriarity. His main desire had always been in anthropology, but he wanted to investigate the land of Froth to the east, and the professor spent his life searching out the history of these islands to the west. Already two very important discoveries were on the verge of being checked out, discoveries that the professor had so desired and so deserved, and yet, these were going to be up to him. How unfair it seemed to him.

"Let's stop here for a few minutes everyone," Kanta said. "But as nice as it seems, don't remove your packs. The cool air will soon stiffen your muscles if we stay too long, and it will make the rest of the trip that much harder. Hang in there, my little ones. The day's journey is soon at end."

They drank deeply from a nearby stream. It was hard to tell if it was the same one that flowed back at the last stop or a new one. As they walked through the forest, the sound of flowing water was heard often, and Kanta followed its course several times. As they drank from it, Bob wondered where its source was and where the flow ended.

It was true what Kanta said. The cool shadows of the forest quickly dried the sweat from their bodies, and a chill was seizing everyone when he beckoned them again to start walking. And just as quickly, the warmth worked back into their muscles as each step followed another. Sometimes the floor sloped upward, almost so gently it was unperceived to the eye, but it was felt by the legs. Each one was glad in Kanta's wisdom to be carrying a walking pole to balance the step and to aid in the movement.

Twice more Kanta stopped them to rest. The talking was held to a minimum as each gladly seized the moment to rest and catch their breath. The travel became slower as fatigue wrapped its grip about each one. And it wasn't the children who first complained of the built up agony, but Nance. But all joined in with agreement.

It was a few minutes more that they marched before Kanta stopped and pointed to a decent size clearing ahead. "Here is where we will camp tonight. There are a couple hours or so of daylight left, but you all have done well, very well."

They stumbled to the clearing, panting and gasping. The packs were slowly peeled off their backs as though painful growths.

"My God!" Nance exclaimed. "I'm so glad to finally stop. I thought I was in great shape, but those last few hundred meters were exhausting. You poor children must be miserable."

"I am tired, mom," Roger answered. "But really, I'm starved."

"Me too!" Sally echoed. "I think I'll go to bed after supper, mom."

"You are all in very good shape," Kanta spoke up. "We traveled as far as I ever took anyone else, and you never complained. The last trip I took involved two young men, both about twenty years old. One whined about the distance we walked and the other about the soreness of his feet and back. The next morning at daybreak, they were both so miserable that we ended up returning to town. I even speeded up my march forcing them to move more quickly. By the time we arrived back in town, they could not move."

He laughed at the thought of it and so did everyone else. Quickly, he gathered up a few long twigs and small vines that were creeping up nearby trees. He called Roger over and gave him directions to follow. Together they soon assembled a makeshift lean-to, but one of surprising strength. By stacking and intertwining twig after twig, and piling leaves upon it by sweeping armful after armful of them that lay nearby, a comfortable shelter was made.

"Dad, mom!" shouted Roger. "Look at what we made. How long do you think we took to make it, huh?"

"Only about ten minutes, son," Bob replied. "That looks pretty good. Do you use this yourself, Kanta?"

"Yes, I do," he replied. "It can even keep the rain off you. Clear out an area there, and Roger and I will make one for you and Mrs. Troyer."

"Can I help too?" Sally replied suddenly with perkiness in her voice.

"You can, my pretty one," Kanta laughed. "Gather many small twigs while Roger and I set up the main structure."

Bob was already clearing out an area and digging a small hole to build a fire in it while Nance started to prepare dough like mixture in a large pot. Kanta had asked the children to continue working on the lean-to. After receiving their instruction on the structure, he left and disappeared into the confines of the forest.

The dry leaves in the hole started to glow, then they burst into flames, and Bob added chips of wood to their flames. Blowing on the flame to aid their combustion, he saw Kanta leave the area. He continued adding larger pieces of wood until a roaring fire was bellowing forth. The heat drove him backward, and he stood up to collect large chunks of wood to keep the fire going.

It was several minutes more before the fire was burning to Bob's satisfaction. He saw that Nance had finished kneading the dough, and the children were standing next to the lean-to they had constructed, laughing with joy of a job well done. He told them to spread their blankets inside one lean-to and his blanket inside the other. And now he wondered where Kanta had gone and why.

His thoughts were answered immediately as Kanta stepped into the camp area with two very large pieces of meat dangling from a rope held in his right hand.

"Rabbits!" he spoke with a large smile. "They were in a trap I had set a few days ago when I planned this trip."

In his left hand was a long straight piece of wood that was stripped of its bark and pointed at one end. With this, he quickly thrust the wood into the rabbits lengthwise. He told Bob and the children to look for two pieces of wood that forked out, which took them only a minute or two.

With little energy, he had the skewered rabbits over the fire. He asked to see the dough that Nance had mixed. Kneeling next to the fire, he scooped out a portion next to the flame and poured the dough into the depression, and then he shoveled part of the hot ashes over the top of the dough. Glancing up, he could see Nance giving Bob a mortified look, while Bob returned the gesture with a shrug.

The children were instructed to take turns turning the meat over the fire, and Nance became busy preparing a pot of coffee. She asked if Kanta enjoyed coffee with his meal or wanted water.

"A nice hot cup of coffee would taste delicious," he responded. "It is one of the few things from the mainland I favor. I understand it is grown in only one area of Victoriana."

"Yes, it is," Nance replied. "In Lukethian, there is a very fertile region where the root is grown. It is then roasted, ground up, and then shipped out to all other areas. We visited that area years ago. It is quite beautiful to see, and if you get the opportunity, Kanta, you should go there. By the way, Kanta, why do you call our mainland Victoriana? I've heard the professor and Bob use it a couple times. In fact, it's not even put into history books that the children use today. Most didn't even have it when I went to school. After all, for the last hundred years or so we have been called the Confederacy. Although, Bob and the professor have made request that schools should make at least mention of the old names our lands have known."

"It is an almost ancient terminology," Bob joined in. "Are you an amateur archeologist or history buff?"

Kanta swept red-hot ashes on top of the ones he poured over the dough and added a couple more sticks of wood to the fire. He placed the pot of coffee Nance had prepared on the other side of the flames to start it to boil. Roger took Sally's place by the fire and began to twist the meat as it slowly sizzled. The campsite soon was filled with the aroma of roast meat and baked bread.

Kanta saw everything was doing fine, then he answered Bob. "There are many things we learn as youngsters from our family that we really don't know the reasons to them. We accept them as fact because they usually come from an elder. My grandfather never called the mainland the Confederacy, but always Victoriana. He told me when his father was a boy that the government would never sanction any permit or activity if Victoriana was written or mentioned. I always thought my ancestors did it mostly out of spite knowing it irritated the officials."

"You are probably right," chuckled Bob. "The government has always felt that it operated best as a united entity, and I agree with them. But the states of Sicatia, Blackroth, Marsalia, and Lakethian once operated as separate countries, or more correctly, kingdoms."

"Don't forget Froth, father!" Roger spoke.

"Yes! Even Froth is part of the Confederacy. Even though we only deal with its western border. Little by little, we are mapping more of it. Did your grandfather ever talk to you about Froth?"

"No, never," Kanta replied. "He said his grandfather would only mention its name with bitterness, and he was going to tell him why when my grandfather got a little older. But he died before my grandfather could be told."

"Kanta! Did your grandfather teach you how to cook bread like that?" Sally spoke as she pointed towards the fire. "It sure seems like a funny way to do it."

"Why, yes he did. And it will soon be done, and you must be as hungry as I am. Go behind those trees and rinse off in the stream. It will be cold but refreshing and by then supper will be ready."

All four of them went to where Kanta pointed and washed themselves in the stream. Just as before, the water was cold, but each one vigorously splashed the cold liquid upon their face, neck, and arms. When they came back to the fireside, Kanta had the meat divided upon metal plates.

He pulled from the ashes the large loaf of bread now done. It looked part gray, part black, and part brown, but when torn in chunks, its aroma was heavenly to the famished campers.

"Don't worry about the crust. Blow away the ash and eat any of it you want. Except for the burnt black part, I eat all of it." Kanta spoke.

"Mmmm!" Nance responded as she pushed a large piece of it in her mouth. "This smells so good. I didn't realize I was so hungry," she mumbled.

"And this meat is so juicy and tender," replied Bob. And all agreed to both comments.

The meal went quickly as their hunger drove them to devour the meat and bread entirely. Kanta brought the pot back from the stream filled with water and set it into the hot coals, and in a few minutes he removed it with its contents warm. He dipped a towel into it and wiped his hands and mouth then dipped the towel back in it. Everyone followed his lead and wiped the grease from hands and face while he poured the steaming coffee into three metal cups.

He handed a cup to Nance and to Bob, then told Roger to go to the stream to fill up the water bag so both children could drink. They all sat drinking, enjoying the quiet as the forest rapidly darkened as the sun's rays no longer penetrated.

After another cup of coffee and a bit of small talk, it was agreed that the time to sleep had come. Bob and Nance crawled into their lean-to, and the children did likewise into theirs. Kanta swept the coals about to spread them, then laid three large logs in a pyramid on top of the coals. Within minutes large flames burst forth bringing warmth into the lean-tos and dancing shadows about the campsite. Kanta bundled his blanket about him and lay near the fire, and soon the flames hypnotic effect lulled everyone into a deep sleep.

At first Bob could not orientate himself to the sound or place as he blinked his eyes several times and tried to focus them. But soon a roaring fire was flashing before him and Kanta's figure could be made out next to it. It was still dark as the smell of coffee drifted his way. As he rolled over and sat up, the stiffness of his body made him groan involuntarily.

The big guide looked his way but showed no expression of acknowledgment. The fire provided enough light for Bob to step about the camp easily, but once he neared the stream, darkness again enveloped him. He knelt down and groped for a secure spot then dipped his hands into the almost frigid water. The cold made him shiver as he washed the sleep from his face. It felt good to enter near the fire, and he poured himself a cup of coffee.

By now the strips of meat Kanta put in the pan were sizzling and sending forth their tantalizing smell. Biscuits were baking in a special pan at the outer fringe of the coals. Kanta unrolled a cloth-covered package to unveil several eggs. "I was afraid these would break before

THE SCROLLS OF BELBOU

I could use them. I wanted especially to surprise the little ones with a good breakfast."

"You are quite a guide, Kanta," Bob spoke with admiration in his voice. "How long have you been up and about?"

"It's been about a half hour or so. As dark as it is now, soon the forest will be light, and the morning chill will be gone once we move on out."

Bob shook the children awake and called over to Nance. While they stumbled about getting their bearings and moving stiffened muscles, he unwrapped a small lantern that was attached to his pack and lit it. He then led the family to the stream where they could wash up. Gasping from the cold, the three scurried ahead of Bob back to the fire, and each child draped a blanket over itself.

Nance marveled at the meal Kanta prepared for them, and was stunned to see him crack eggs into the pan. The delicious smell further awakened everyone, and breakfast was easily consumed. Just before they finished eating, dawn came upon the forest and filled their hearts with joy for the new day.

The camp was quickly cleared up as packs were reassembled and the gear wrapped up after being cleaned. The fire was snuffed out by a bucket of water, and its ashes were mixed about to insure no spark remained. Refreshed and well fed now, the group moved onward, deeper into the forest.

It was about a half-hour later when Kanta beckoned them to stop and rest. "We are less than a hour away," Kanta remarked.

"The professor thought he discovered what would be paths leading us to the cottage you have visited. Are there such paths or was he imagining or hoping for them?" asked Bob.

"Because the professor knows that I venture often deep into this forest, he too mentioned what he found," answered Kanta. "Such findings allowed me to locate the cottage," he continued. "But soon I will let you decide just what those findings may be."

Several minutes more of walking passed, then Kanta stopped. He stood silent and looked at Bob and questioned, "Where do you want us to go? I will let you lead now."

Bob looked puzzled for a moment, then brightened. He looked about him and at first saw nothing to give him guidance. Suddenly, the area did look slightly different. The trees were no longer so random even though they were as numerous. There was an area that had no trees. Casually looking at it, one could easily have it blend with the forest, but looking for it, one could see the trees forming a corridor, the undergrowth withheld its tunnel effect. And the growth of bushes and grasses tended to flow from the edges into the middle.

Bob knelt down and rubbed into the ground. Quickly, he scampered several meters along this area. "Why it's very hard in the middle area and a normal texture on the edges," he exclaimed. "Can we spend anytime checking this area out, Kanta?"

"Not now," Kanta replied. "I will tell you this ... that I dug up part of this kind of area and there is a layer of gravel inches below the surface. And there are at least three more such paths leading out from the cottage."

"Then he was right," Bob excitedly spoke. "These are roads in the forest. If what you say is true, Kanta, then not only were they well built, but they were well used. To be pounded so hard as to deny trees from forming over God knows how long, why a multitude had to travel over them continuously for some time."

Faintly, the outline of a path appeared to them and weaved past some trees. "It's like looking at an outline. Once you see it then it's easy to see, but my God, you could stand two meters from it and not see it," shouted Bob as he walked a few steps onward.

"No wonder no mention of such a path was ever told to us. Come on everyone! We are going for a little hike."

Excitedly, they formed a line and marched onward. "Do you know what luck this is?" Bob asked. "Everything fell into place for us, the lighting, the time of day."

"Not to mention being led right to it by Kanta, dear," Nance reminded Bob.

"Oh, I know. But not even the professor spoke of this path with such clarity."

"It's kind of weird if you ask me," Nance replied.

"I'm kind of scared, daddy," Sally cried out.

"OH! You always are scared," Roger said as he bravely moved next to his dad to help him lead the way.

The path became broken here and there, but a few steps or so soon found them moving along its course again. It was also moving them deeper into the forest.

"If it wasn't such a sunny morning, the light filtering into this growth wouldn't be as clear," Nance spoke out. "You know, I turn my head sometimes and I lose sight of the trail. It's here and yet it isn't."

Suddenly, they came upon it. It was a clearing with a large cottage. The suddenness of it stopped them in their tracks, then slowly they moved closer to the building. Turning about here and there, this way and that way, they moved with wonder.

"All the literature I've read never mentioned this," Nance seemed to whisper through pursed lips.

The air seemed clear and crisp, yet there seemed to be a feeling of mystery about it. A sense of antiquity was about the place that made each one shiver. The clearing was not smooth, by far, for there were high weeds and bushes about the place. Yet, there indeed was a clearing right there amidst the forest. And the cottage loomed before them.

"The ground here is like the path, it feels super hard for there does seem to be a base of gravel packed underneath," Bob said as he knelt on the ground and picked away with a piece of stone.

"That explains why the cottage hasn't been surrounded by trees but by this smaller growth," Nance replied while walking up to the doorway. "Shall we go in?"

With a hard shove from Bob and Kanta, the heavy door gave way slightly, and with repeated shoves, it slowly swung open. Before them was a big room, and the eye was drawn to the big fireplace in the middle wall straight ahead. In front of the fireplace was a huge table with three large chairs and a group of several pots for cooking on the other side. The furniture was constructed of heavy wood now layered with a heavy coat of dust and cobwebs.

Looking about the room, it was apparent no one had been here for a long time. Sealed off in a forest, it was difficult to tell whether years, decades, or even centuries had passed since the last occupant was here. To the left of the fireplace was another door, and all advanced to it. With several grunts, Roger tried to push it open.

"Son! It swings out," laughed Bob and the others. But it took several tugs from Bob and Roger to even start the door open. Then slowly it yielded to their pull and was soon wide open.

It was dark inside, but the light through the doorway revealed a window straight ahead but blocked by a wooden shutter. Knocking the latch that held it, Bob swung the heavy wooded cover to one side and light flew in, a welcome guest to the dark. It was a room about five meters square, mostly barren except for large wall shelves on one side. On the shelves were what appeared to be tubular leather casings.

"What luck! There are large candles in these pouches," cried Bob as he popped a covering off one. "Nance, get a couple of these things going and rip the picnic sheet up to use as dust cloths. Let's clean this place up. It looks like we'll be here for a while."

Turning to leave, Nance commanded, "Well then, you and Roger see if that fireplace is in working order. It would be nice to have a big fire going ... not only to warm us, but to burn off the mustiness of this place. Kanta, please use a couple of those pots and bring us water."

Quickly, everyone went to clear and clean up the room with Bob and Roger attacking the fireplace. "Roger, you'll have to climb the roof to see if anything is blocking the chimney. I can't see any light." Bob called out as he leaned into the grate while trying to peer up into the chimney. "And be careful when you get up there."

"Dad! Dad! You were right," Roger's voice filtered down the chimney several minutes later. "There was a large board and a brick on top of it. The board was almost rotted through, though. I thought I was going to drop this brick down on you."

"It looks darn good considering it has been who know how long since it has been used," replied Bob. "I'll be out to help gather some wood with you, Roger."

"Well, it's going to be impossible without soap and lots of water to clean this place decently. Sally and I are going to concern ourselves only with the table, chairs, bench, and the area around it," Nance exclaimed while Bob walked out the door.

Wood that was lying about was gathered and brought into the house, and soon a fire was blazing away. The cleanup was attacked with frenzy. No words had to be spoken when Nance finally laid out the food on the table. It had been hours since they found the cottage and now famished bodies eagerly lunged at the food. The roaring fire and food gave contentment to the entire group.

Roger got up and wondered into the small room while the remaining food was being collected and put away. Bob took out his pipe and in seconds had smoke pouring out of its bowl. It had been days since he last smoked his favorite tobacco and he just idled away a few minutes enjoying this simple act. Looking about him, he pensively spoke," I wonder how long this place has been here? And I wonder how long has it been since anyone had lived here."

"Our teacher has mentioned these islands but said nothing of importance has ever been found here. Jackie Doblin, who sits two seats behind me was going to do a report on some legend he read about but never got to give it because he came down with the flu," Sally exclaimed.

"Dad! Dad! These don't seem to be as heavy as the other pouches with candles in them," cried Roger, as he carried in a large pouch similar to the others ones they had recently emptied.

Bob hoisted the pouch up then down. There was a leather cord holding it closed which he pulled apart. Inside were individual leather cases. Etched on each lid was a number, and laying the cases out, they numbered eight.

"Good God," whispered Bob. "These are some kind of scrolls."

Silently, all watched as he sorted them out in a numerical sequence composed of slashes. He twisted the lid of one until it became free. "These seem to have been sealed with a wax," he grunted.

Slowly and gently he tapped the bottom end, and an oiled parchment scroll came forth. As if holding a precious jewel, he unrolled what were several sheets. There before them words became unveiled, words that waited from an ancient history to be exposed to the eye of man.

Shaking slightly. Bob Troyer gazed upon the parchment. "The writing is so vivid," he whispered in awe inspired tone.

"Can you read them, father?" Sally excitedly cried out. And they all leaned toward him, even Kanta listened with a gaze of rapture.

"My God! These words are in a dead language we use in our sciences. We stumbled on a historical link. My heart is racing just gazing upon this," Bob stammered. "Let me get my thinking cap on, it's been a while, but I always loved reading this language. If only the professor was here. Not only would he be enthralled, but he knows this language better than anyone."

"Read it, daddy, read it," Sally squealed. And each person squirmed into a comfortable position awaiting the story. Slowly, almost reverently, Bob Troyer began.

SCROLL I

My name is Belbou, the crippled one. It was by accident of birth which caused my left arm to be lame, but an accident that has allowed me to become chief scribe to Anasha, the king's physician and sorcerer. This is his cottage, and it is here where most of my writing is done. My work is to keep the records of the court when in session, but when our visits bring us here, Anasha allows me to write this diary. His reflections are often deep and his countenance most foreboding these last few months. He encourages me to keep up my evening writings for he has more than once conveyed to me that these words might one day be all that remains of our glorious kingdom. This responsibility weighs heavy upon me. What he means or how he knows is but a mystery. But one thing I do know Anasha is always right.

I live during the glorious reign of our good king, Bathen. We are truly blessed subjects, for as he grows older, his wisdom grows greater, as does his love for prince Abrams, his grandson. And it is prince Abrams who is chosen to be our next monarch, for his father, prince Asher, has been taken by the evil Malechar, and no one yet knows what has become of him.

My court records will be able to tell anyone who reads them all about our life here in our glorious Eden. They reflect on daily matters, and I even included the fashion of dress, and what is expected of whom and when during court sessions. Though I must add, lord Anasha frowns on these frivolous additions. However, I will not dwell much on such matters here and will commence into what has happened but a few months ago until now. Events have been happening to make our kingdom topsy-turvy, and but by a stunning miracle, I would not be here alive to register it. This story of my king and his people... I must not let it die... it must not vanish. Let me now start from the beginning of the events...

We are the people of Eden, and our principality encompasses five islands, with Eden as the heart. The other four islands are called Queenland, Boxer, Greenborough, and Pliney. We now stand alone against the evil forces of Malechar, who this very day is supreme conqueror of the mainland, Victoriana. And who now is gathering forces to subdue us. Parts of his army have already gained position on each of the other islands, and because of this extremely sudden and bold move, chaos has gripped our kingdom.

The forces of Malechar that have landed on the other islands are really not large in number. But the very fact that invasion is upon each one with such suddenness prevented proper reaction by our forces. Almost all of the islands' warriors have fled their area to gather here in Eden. We have become truly an island psychologically as well as physically. In fact, Malechar's men invaded our island, too, but the swift response of prince Asher repelled those forces. However, in the fighting that ensued, the prince was captured and taken back with the invading forces. The loss of such a brave and intelligent leader can only deepen our concern and make our enemy more confident. No one has heard of his well being, so worry weighs even heavier on our good king for his son.

But now all wait to assume their orders from king Bathen, and the court is filled with the officers of our army and the leader of our islands.

"Captain Booter! What has the king decided to do? Is there any word of the families left behind on the other islands, especially Greensborough?" A voice cried out above the din as the chief captain entered the room.

"Gentlemen, gentlemen! Please settle down and we will discuss the situation at hand as we know it. I just left the council of king Bathen and lord Anasha. Soon they should be here and answer any questions," boomed Michael Booter.

He was an imposing figure standing before the assembly. He was a soldier for the king, but also his trusted aide, and now second in command after the king. No one feared this situation, for his wisdom and kindness matched his prowess as a master warrior skilled in the sword, lance, and bow. The soldiers from all ranks listened and obeyed willingly to this man, for they also knew he was open to all manner of conversation, whether it was an idea from the lowest ranking man to a complaint from any officer. He was their direct link to the king himself.

"What does Anasha plan to do? No trickery or mystical potion will repel Malechar and his men," shouted a stout officer standing in the rear of the room. And murmur chorused his reply. "Is it wise to include him in the councils of war?"

"For shame, Mr. Grove, you should know what wisdom and strength Anasha has, for I have listened to him, as well we all have, since we can remember. And especially in these trying times he has countered the king's and my arguments with views we did not see. Anasha is one of our greatest assets against Malchar, for as long as I can remember his announcements have always been true." And at Captain Booter's reply the murmuring stopped.

In that instant, the king himself and Anasha entered the great hall. All bowed respectfully to the old king, and he acknowledged them with a nod of his head. His face seemed especially weary, and the lines of his craggy face were deeper than they were weeks ago. His hair was silver from years of living and years of ruling. He was deeply loved by his subjects, for his reign was essentially peaceful and fruitful. In his early days his courage and fighting skill prevented a skirmish on the mainland from becoming a major war that threatened the islands of our kingdom.

King Bathen also reflected great pride towards his kingdom and its people. He was stern to all who broke our law but much sterner to foreigners who would make actions which demeaned us or threatened us. Travelers to Victoriana from our islands were treated respectfully and with dignity because of his wise rule. And those who visited us praised our way of life that under our king and his predecessors allowed more independence and liberty than those five states that make up the mainland.

Prince Asher, Bathen's son, was trained from birth for his responsibilities to take over the reign of his father. Wisely, through Anasha's guidance, the training involved learning to fight, and to know court etiquette, but he had to spend months by living with various families, learning the basis of the trades each one had to offer. By this means, the prince became aware of his future subjects, their thoughts, dreams, hopes, strengths, and weaknesses. It was by this means that king Bathen was trained, and the king saw the wisdom of it and sent his son through the same educational process.

But now prince Asher was captive, and everyone knew the pain the good king must feel. He had served the people well, and the common feeling amongst all was to serve the king in the most trying time in our recorded history.

"Officers and members of the court, each one of you know the meaning of this gathering. Let us therefore do away with normal proceedings and let every man here speak what is on his mind or in his heart," proclaimed the king. "But before any questions are asked, let me bring all here up to date on what is happening. Even though we have been caught off guard by Malechar's boldness, our spies on the continent have been reporting in to us along with our people from the other islands through carrier birds. So we do know somewhat of the devil's intention, Good Anasha, feel free to interrupt and answer me and anyone."

And with this statement, Anasha bowed and moved forward to stand next to his king now sitting on the throne facing all about him. And now king Bathen began on the events that had happened.

"About three years ago from the far eastern state of Froth, Malechar came out of nowhere. We do not know as of yet whether he was a native of Froth, or of any other state, or from the areas we call the lost regions. But he seized power in Froth and developed a well-organized base. After the mysterious and sudden death of king Victor, the ninth, who kept the continent under a relatively united rule, no one really came forth to seize control. His son, Luther, tried to bring about control of the five states, but the dukes who willingly followed Luther's father now bickered amongst themselves and the people."

The king paused and took a drink that had been handed to him and then he continued. "There was a great convention called where all the leaders assembled for the purpose of ending the strife. Under king Victor and his father, and his father too, the people became accustomed to more of a united kingdom, much in line as ours, and peace reigned, and with it a stable economy developed. Though the continent was comprised of five distinct states, each one ruled by a separate royal family, each family was related in one way or another, and they accepted one head to rule over them. This king was chosen from the family of Orange in the state of Sicatia. By superior forces and sheer personality, the king, Iron Blade, dominated the states of Sicatia, Marsalia, and Lakethian. The states of Froth to the east and Blackroth to the north sued for peace and accepted the leadership of the Orange family. Surprisingly, over the following six decades, it became accepted by most that the royal lineage from Sicatia would rule. And over the rule of the last two kings, the continent became known totally as Victoriana, after the second queen, Victoria. But now with no leadership over the states these last three years, restlessness and turmoil have developed between the royal families, and between the people who yearn for guidance. Sadly, mistrust and scheming between the families have developed... "

And now Anasha stepped forward and addressed the assembly. "We always have had some of our people on the continent to report to us on whatever events that might seem important to us. For several years this seemed like a useless idea, but now great benefits are being reaped from our good king's prudence on the concept. Though events of recent doings have swiftly paralyzed us momentarily, our agents are quickly reporting in or have sent messages to us on what is happening. Be of good cheer guardians of this island. We will not send you into battle completely shrouded from information. Sire, please continue."

After a long pause, king Bathen continued. "The convention only caused greater rift and confusion. But one thing came out of it, and that was the personage of Malechar. By dividing the royal families at the convention, he was able to divide whatever wise counsel they could give by working together. It was by false promises to each that he gained their confidence, and finally by intimidation that he acquired total rule of the continent."

He took another long drink from the cup he held and sighed, then he continued. "He has raised a powerful army from this seizure. At first, he used it to squash any opposition until his rule was secure against the five royal families, then he quelled any open dissension, for although the people fear and obey him, they despise him, too. There is no love for him, his rule is held together by sheer fear."

"Sire!" A voice called out. "How did he raise such an army? There was none so large before his rule."

Moving his head to catch a glimpse of the man, the king answered. "Every family with a son had to give his son in service to Malechar. Every family with no son, the husband had to serve him. Any deviation or dissent meant death to the whole family. Such is his evil way, and by this way he plans to conquer this world of ours."

Then Anasha spoke to the assembly in order to relieve the tired king. "This threat on each family is the strength of his recruitment, but it is his weakness, also. Surely the defeat of Malechar would cause a rapid deterioration of his forces. But, alas, my good people, these poor soldiers are captained by Malechar's own chosen men from the region of Froth. From this area also comes his own personal bodyguard. It is a regiment of hardened military men highly skilled in war and destruction. They have no comprehension of fair play. Defeat isn't their goal but total destruction. It is these men who fight directly with Malechar, and these types hold his army together."

"Tell us, Anasha, do you know their number?" Cried a man near the front.

"And do they match us in fighting technique?" asked another.

Anasha hesitated, then looked at the king. Bathen shook his head sadly and spoke. "Hold nothing back, Anasha. If these men are to fight and perhaps die, let them know what they are to face."

The hall became filled with low murmuring, then it quieted as Anasha answered. "Brave men of our beloved Eden, yours is a hard task ahead, but not impossible. Malechar fights to conquer, you fight to live. He will know of your courage and skill."

Again the voices of the men came forth as they pondered Anasha's statement. But king Bathen raised himself from his seat and quiet was restored. "This personal army of his is formidable," the king spoke. "It numbers from ten to twelve thousand strong. Each is well trained for the sword and bow."

A chorus of cheers rang forth, for indeed if equal in number, each felt confident in victory. After several minutes of such confident unity, the king again signaled for silence and spoke. 'Were it so equal, my dear subjects, I would rejoice with you, and I know no known army can stand before you in victory. But these men are not only well trained and vicious, but by some mysterious force or spell or whatever it is that Malechar commands, each soldier seems to have the force of ten men when they fight under his banner and guidance."

Visibly shaking, the king sat down and Anasha continued. "What we are dealing with is a very evil person shielded by an evil force. His army is mortal all right, but should he attack us personally, and we have every reason to believe he will, it will be as though fighting a force of one hundred thousand or more."

Captain Booter quickly spoke. "Good Anasha, how long do we have before Malechar invades us?"

"A week to ten days. Any more would be a blessing, but reliable sources report he is massing along the northwest coast of Sicatia. The only thing preventing him from invading us now is in the collecting of the necessary barges from all along the coast to transport his troops. Many brave people have sabotaged their own barges, and it has cost them their lives and the lives of their families to buy us this precious time."

King Bathen stood up and shouted. "We are facing a very evil force. If I knew there was no hope, I would capitulate now. It would mean the destruction of Eden's royal family. But who would be spared?" He faced them and added sternly. "I would capitulate now. But even this act would not satisfy Malechar. We are the only hope the world has to stand against him. I, for one, would rather go down fighting for we all must die anyway."

They cheered the brave words of the king and knew if what he said was true, then death awaited all. One man yelled for quiet, the asked. "Anasha! Is there nothing you can do against Malechar? Can not your sorcery combat his? Are there no words of encouragement you can give us?"

Anasha stood without uttering a word for several moments. Just as the uneasiness grew from his silence, he answered. "I have tried to serve you all well for these many years. My life has been my duty to king Bathen and to his father. I had hoped even to his son, but even without Malechar, the years flow swifter upon my body and my time draws near to leave this service. Perhaps what he controls is from ancient legend, and from ancient legend I must seek to deal with him. But I do not know if I have enough time."

He walked over to the throne and turned back to the crowd. "I do not have any words of encouragement that can stop an arrow or shield a sword. I do know this, everything has its time, be it good or be it evil. Be thou patient and understanding to stand strong against evil and to do your duty for good."

With this, Anasha slowly walked away into the other chamber. The king stood and all bowed before him. He, also, followed into the other room. Captain Booter told each to encourage their companies and platoons when they returned, and to double the sea wall watch. Such went the court meeting as our beloved island prepared for war.

SCROLL II

Anasha informed the king that he wanted to go to his cottage. It was there that Anasha hoped to discover some way to combat the evil Malechar, and it was there where his books, potions, and instruments were normally stored. It was not uncommon for Anasha to go there and stay months at a time, for he enjoyed the peace of the forest and its tranquillity from court life. But now the time for leisure was past, and perhaps the fate of Eden lay in what he could discover.

It was almost midsummer now, and the cool surroundings of the cottage would feel good to the old physician. King Bathen also enjoyed his visits there, and he decided that he would go with Anasha to the cottage. He wanted to take young prince Abrams and Captain Booter's son, Andrew, with him. He wanted to spend what could be his last visit with his dear friend, and his last visit with the prince. He ensured Anasha that it would be for two nights and one day only, but that the two boys were to stay with Anasha. The king felt that when the fighting broke out, the boys would be much safer under Anasha's care deep in the sanctuary of the forest.

Prince Abrams and his friend Andrew were as two brothers since birth. It was rare to see them separated, and each lived in the other's home, welcomed and treated as family. The prince was the oldest, and he would be thirteen by summer's end, while Andrew had turned twelve in the spring. But Andrew was equal in height and weight to the prince, and both bloodied each other many times in their play. Each carried himself with a prideful posture, and it was easy to tell that they belonged to the life of the court.

It was great joy that Abrams felt when he heard he could spend time with his grandfather. Since his father's capture, he would slip into depression for short intervals, and the king was very busy to spend time with him It was only with Andrew that he felt relief from his loss.

The king's heart was heavy with grief. His son, Asher, had given him so much pride and joy. Since the death of his queen four years ago, he had been drawn so close to his son and grandson. Now with Asher gone, his world seemed more torn apart than united. If only he knew whether his son was alive and well could there be comfort. He told Captain Booter that he could accept his son's death, but it was the uncertainty of Asher's existence that plagued him so. Would Malechar torture Asher or enslave him with degrading or perverted treatment? Such thoughts piled on top of thoughts of war against his beloved kingdom gave great stress and worry to the king. He knew the royal families of the continent and many of their friends well. There were many reports of cruelty to them in order to rule the continent, and this too saddened him.

It was with such sadness that the king's life was enveloped. Thus, Anasha did not offer any opposition to his king. Such a diversion could give him strength for the following days ahead. And the joy his grandson gave him would be a tonic to further rejuvenate the wise king. From such turmoil and dejection, a respite was needed, so the trip was planned.

Princess Sara, Asher' wife, made sure all was packed for Abrams's trip. The prince was her only treasure left for the concern over Asher kept her melancholy ever since. She, too, loved the king, and to him was very much a daughter. It was with sadness to see Abrams leave, but also with relief to know he would be with Anasha. She looked on with pride watching her son and his grandfather ride up to her upon their steeds.

She kissed the king's hand and bid him well. But when the young prince bent down to kiss her, her tears flowed freely. "My lord," she cried. "Here is my treasure and I am missing you both already."

"I have always loved you for your gentle heart, Sara," the king responded. "He is a fine sapling of a man, and he shall do us proud. Now we must go for Anasha waits down the road. Besides, I must not let the people see my tears which would surely fall were I to stay here any longer."

Next to them, Andrew's mother was hugging her son and kissing him unashamedly. After a hug from his father, he swung upon his saddle.

"Tell me, son," captain Booter inquired. "What shall be your business on this trip?"

"To guard and protect prince Abrams, father," Andrew responded.

"Aye!" Booter spoke. "And what is your responsibility?"

"To do my duty towards my king and for my country," the boy replied. "But I shall miss you, father. You must lead the army into battle and you will probably die." And tears came forth from the boy.

"Aye!" Captain Booter replied. "And when I am killed in battle, what should be said of me?"

"That he did his duty. That he feared not doing his duty more than cold or hunger, more than torture or pain, more than death itself."

"You have learned it well, my son. When your time comes, let it also be said of you."

Looking at the sadness of his son, Captain Booter soothingly continued. "What I do I choose to do. Just remember, when one does his duty well, usually everything works out ... even in death. Let not death frighten you, my son. Fear not doing your duty more."

The king, his grandson, and Andrew rode up to where Anasha awaited them. At his side were four soldiers from the king's bodyguard. Normally, the king and his family traveled freely about the kingdom, but now Captain Booter, with Anasha's approval, created a company of soldiers strictly to guard the royal family and their castle. This four was assigned to ride with the king. Two rode ahead about one hundred meters while the other two stayed about fifty meters behind as rear guards. It was this royal entourage that traveled into the forest to Anasha's cottage, along with myself, Belabou, the scribe.

The king and Anasha rode closer together so that they could discuss matters. There was no protocol between the two during such gatherings or in private council. Bathen was king for over forty years now, and Anasha was his physician, sorcerer, and teacher since the king's boyhood days when even Bathen's father depended on Anasha. Never did the king feel such peril to his kingdom as now. It deeply concerned him for his subjects' welfare, but also saddened him that perhaps soon he and Anasha would be forever parted. As for Anasha, whatever grief he felt or concerns he had were not perceived in his features or words.

The king also recalled his childhood days and the joy he had of them. Often, he would look over to the prince and Andrew, watching them as they bantered back and forth, oblivious to the impending danger. He laughed when he recalled the pranks he and his good friend, William, did as young boys. William was Andrew's grandfather, and the king marveled at the cyclic manner of things. The memory of his good and dear friend always was with him, and the deed that brought his death lived with him, too. Now his grandson and William's grandson played about him, and he wondered would duty to him or to his grandson bring about Andrew's demise as it did to William. Such thoughts he had as they journeyed into the forest.

SCROLL III

It was in the waning hours of the afternoon when they approached the cottage. The trip seemed to have taken minutes rather than hours, for the beauty of the woods and the conversation seemed to have slowed the passing of time. The fireplace was soon roaring with flame, and supper was quickly prepared by one of the guards.

They all sat together to eat, for the king enjoyed the conversation of all men, and he asked each of the guards about their lives. It was rare, indeed, for the king after such a long reign not to be able to recognize each of his subjects. To alienate the royal family from its subjects was long ago considered unwise, and such consideration endeared king to commoner, commoner to king. What fascinated most travelers from the continent was the ease of royalty and subjects together, and that the good king knew the names of almost all the people. Once introduced by name, the king remembered it and used this courteous manner in all his dealings. But the respect and conduct of each to the other still followed a defined protocol. The subjects knew their station and honored the royal lineage, and in return, this line was taught the great responsibility for honest and fair rule.

As darkness descended upon the forest, the guards secured the area and agreed amongst themselves the posting of a guard and whose turn it should be next. Anasha ordered the two boys to clear the dishes away and to clean them. He also ordered them to bed after those duties were done.

Anasha then poured two goblets of a special wine he kept in the wine racks, and he offered one to the king. They talked of the possible landing areas where Malechar and his army might attack. What worried the two was the power this strange army possessed under this evil man. The king's spies on the continent indicated that their number equaled the forces king Bathen could muster to repel them. But as Anasha mentioned before the assembly, an evil force seemed to provide each of Malechar's men with terrifying power. When they fought against the army forces on the continent, it seemed to have taken several decided blows to kill one of these men. When Anasha mentioned that perhaps each man fought as ten, he felt no exaggeration in this. He wondered how he could combat such a force, and he was afraid he would not have the time to do it.

But both agreed that whatever place Malechar would attack, the place would be known in advance, and that Captain Booter would have the army well prepared for battle. They left the tactics to him, knowing there was none other more capable.

The pounding of a horse's hooves broke the calm of the night, and a guard escorted the rider into the room.

"What brings you here in such haste in the dark of night?" questioned the king. "I fear that the invasion is upon us."

"Sire!" the rider panted. "Captain Booter bid me haste to bring you this message."

The rider gave the paper to the king. With trembling hands, he broke the seal and read it. As he gazed about the room tears flowed from his eyes. The rider and guard turned their heads away so as to ease the king's feelings.

"Is it bad news, sire?" Anasha inquired.

"My son lives, Anasha, my son lives," the words poured forth. "He was seen last night in the prison at Blackroth's castle. Our contact talked to him and all is well. They have not harmed him. Nothing more was said, but we know he is alive."

The king seized the wine bottle and poured five more goblets and handed one to each guard and the rider. "A toast to Prince Asher," he shouted.

"To Prince Asher!" responded each man.

The rider was offered a plate of meat and bread, and the king sat next to the five to read the message again. Prince Abrams sat at his side, and it was good to see the joy that each one showed. After several minutes, the king took the prince back to bed. He then poured himself another drink and bid Anasha to join him in this happy hour.

The old physician declined the offer of drink, and after several more minutes of conversation told the king that he wanted to do some reading. Downing the last drop, the king stood up to go to bed.

"Tell me, Anasha," he asked. "This news gladdens my heart, but hold nothing back. What do you suppose he wants with my son? Could he want ransom?"

"It could be ransom, my lord," Anasha answered. "But I don't think so. His ransom would not be money, for he doesn't need it. The only ransom he would ask for Prince Asher would be capitulation of your kingdom...a price you could not pay, nor would your son expect you to pay."

"Well, why is he holding him prisoner in Blackroth castle? The castle of Orange in Sicatia would surely do. Does he expect us to attack him and free my son there?"

"That is not a bad idea," mused Anasha. "But what I am afraid of is that he holds the prince in Blackroth to eventually move him into Froth. From there, we might never hear of him again."

"A terrible thought, indeed," the king spoke. "Our hands seem tied right now to the impending invasion. But for now, let me rejoice in this first good news in a long time." With that remark, Bathen yawned a mighty yawn. "Good night, Anasha," he spoke. "May you find us a solution to this dilemma. I fear this task is too great even for your mighty skill and wisdom, though you will do your best." And with this, he half-staggered to his bed and was soon asleep.

I, Belabou, then watched as Anasha lifted a secret panel on the floor and pulled out a large chest. With a loud grunt, he pried open its lid and pulled out several old looking scrolls that I never saw before in all my years with him. He gathered them upon his writing table, and after lighting another candle, he sat before them and began reading. It was after many minutes that I fell asleep at my desk even as the old man read on into the night.

It was the sound of a guardsman stirring the ashes in the fireplace that awoke me. After stretching and yawning to brush the sleep from myself, my eyes focused on my master still at the table. He often would go several days on little or no sleep. I believe it was the concoction he was always drinking that allowed him to do so, Still, I marveled at his ability to stay up for such long periods. Earlier in my service to him, I feared for his health, but he never appeared for the worse. I must say such habits allowed him to do much reading, writing, and dabbling at experiments that I know nothing about, nor would I have the nerve to ask. My place in his service is to write the records of the court, and when with Anasha, to administer to his personal requests.

Soon, the king staggered into the room holding his head and groaning followed by the two boys. "I am not use to more than a glass or two of wine. AYIEE! My head throbs," he moaned. "Anasha, do you have any medicine for this?"

If Anasha seemed perturbed by all this commotion in his house, he did not show it, but he arose and opened a cupboard. He dumped a spoon of white powder into a cup of water and mixed it. "It will be bitter," he said. "But drink it all and soon you'll feel better." The king gulped it down at once. With a look of disgust, he told Anasha he wasn't sure if the cure was worth it.

Everyone sat down for breakfast, and by the time it was finished, even king Bathen felt much better. Plans for hunting were made by the boys, and the mood became joyous. It had been over a year since the king had gone hunting with his grandson, and Anasha smiled to see Bathen's enjoyment, and he knew it was good for the king to escape from the everyday pressure of his labor.

It was decided that the hunt would be done on foot, and all joined in except Anasha, Belabou, and a guard. The guard was to stay to care for the horses and to help Belabou chop and stack wood to be used during the next couple weeks. Anasha waved to them as the hunters disappeared into the forest, and then he went back to his reading.

The day passed quickly, and in the late afternoon the hunting party returned tired but happy. The forest held many different species of animals, and the favorite of the hunters was the small deer and the rabbit. Seven rabbits had been killed and two deer. Bathen was extremely pleased to have killed one deer and the boys the other, and it was with robust cheerful talking that the animals were dressed.

The meat for dinner was cut and put on the fire while the rest was placed in a small shed used for smoking and drying meat. It would be this meat that Anasha and his guests would use for later. The meal was rapidly consumed by all, as no one lacked an appetite.

By the time the cleanup was finished, darkness was well upon them. The young prince and Andrew went to bed with no hesitation. One guard posted himself outside the door while the others bedded down by their campfire several meters from the cottage.

The king lit his pipe, and he and Anasha talked for about a hour more. Bathen questioned Anasha on what was possibly found to help the kingdom. But, alas, Anasha informed him that nothing he read so far was of any use. Anasha also told him that he had much reading to do, and at this, the king did not let any depression grip him. On this night, even Anasha blew out his candles and joined everyone for sleep.

The night flew by as each dwelled in deep slumber. And as the day began, the mood was more sober than yesterday's. King Bathen knew how little time he had spent with his grandson, and how he loved him so. Now he must part from him this morning, and only providence knew if and when they would meet again.

The boys chattered openly and still bragged about their hunting exploits while eating breakfast. Their mood was joyful, and they seemed unaware of the seriousness of the events that were ahead. But quickly it was over, and as the guards prepared the horses for the journey back, the king gathered his grandson into his arms and set Andrew next to his side.

"I must go back to court now," he spoke softly. "I shall miss you both very much."

He drew Abrams close and patted him upon the head. After several moments of silence, he released his hug and spoke. "You are the last direct line of the royal family, Abrams. I expect you to obey Anasha here. He will be busy, but for safety's sake, I want you and you, Andrew, to stay here. Should any strange events occur, you may have to follow him to a special place deeper into the forest."

"We will fight to the last, grandfather!" Abrams loudly proclaimed.

"And, I sir, will protect the prince," Andrew joined in.

At this, the king chuckled. "I know you will, Andrew." He turned to Anasha who was standing by the doorway watching them. "Anasha! Did you ever see such brave lads? Why, what enemy would ever dare to attack us when we have such bravery in our midst. But first, your duty will be to live so Eden will have a king to follow. After all, who will lead them?"

Tears started to flow from the prince as he hugged his grandfather. "Oh grandfather," he cried. "I am frightened that I will never see you again. You are the king. I don't want to rule. I want you."

Andrew turned his head so the king could not see his tears, and he quickly wiped his nose on his sleeve. The king tousled the boy's hair. "Andrew! I have known your father since he was a boy like you are now. A finer man there could never be, and the kingdom stands ready to fight under his command. I know you will take good care of Abrams. But your duty, and yours my young prince, is to stay here and obey Anasha. And should the need arrive .... " Here he hesitated, then continued. "Should the need arrive, you are to flee where Anasha will take you. The forest is our friend and ally, and I know you will be protected by it."

He kissed both boys and stood up. "I know you will take care of them, of all of us, Anasha," he spoke. "I will leave you one of the guards to help you and to use as a courier. There will be a constant messenger relay between us. I will send one to you daily. If an emergency arises, I will use the birds."

Anasha nodded his head then stood before the king and bowed deeply. Bathen seized him by the arm and hugged him deeply. Without delay, he mounted his horse and was on his way. The four riders gave a quick wave, and Anasha, prince Abrams, and Andrew stood in the doorway and watched until all were gone from view.

After a few minutes of silence and uneasiness, the two boys were ordered to exercise the horses briefly, rub them down, and feed them. Later, Anasha told them, they could do whatever they wanted to do as long as they stayed within hearing distance of his horn.

They soon became engrossed in their chore, and Anasha resumed his study of the ancient scrolls. He looked older than ever before, and often he would gaze out the window for long periods of time. I worried about my master, for I have never seen him so forlorn in all my service to him.

The next week passed quickly and uneventfully. As the king mentioned, daily a rider from the court would come, usually in the evening, then leave at daybreak with whatever Anasha cared to tell him. The news was good in the sense that no enemy had been sighted. On the seventh day, the courier mentioned that reports from the continent were aware of the evil Malechar massing his bodyguard for invasion within a day or so. Eden's entire army was gathered together at the castle awaiting the lookout's report on where the invasion would take place.

SCROLL IV

I, Belabou, write this scroll and parts of others with some liberty. That which I witness is written down as absolute, for it is from that which I have seen or heard. Other aspects of these scrolls are from reliable accounts told to me from those who are invisible, mainly the servants of those whom I talk about. They move in and out of their masters lives basically unseen, treated as though they were a piece of furniture. The actions and words of their masters do not change in their presence because to their masters they offer no threat. But, by these servants, my story can be told with more detail. As I am a servant, too, they have freely imparted what they have seen to me, just as I impart what I see to you.

So, thusly, I can continue my story as though I, Belabou, have witnessed these events

Nailock walked rapidly to the place where Malechar was seated. "My lord," he shouted. "The fleet has finally been gathered and secured. We await only your word to start the invasion."

Malechar smiled and chuckled with a wicked laugh. He stood up and smacked his right fist into his other hand. He was an imposing figure standing well over two meters with broad shoulders and heavy strong legs and arms. But it was his face that possessed others to fear him. His eyes were very dark, almost black, which shone fiercely. They always have a sinister glow about them, and they gleamed an evil stare.

Coupled with a darkened complexion and heavy beard trimmed very, very short, his countenance excreted terror and horror to those who displeased him. Only Nailock, his commander of the bodyguard, and Hawthorne, his second -in -command failed to tremble in his presence. And of this fear, he made great use of it.

"At last!" he bellowed. "At last! When we conquer Mylako, we will have all of Eden. Only they remain between me and the rule of this world."

He swept his tunic across his shoulders and walked over to the window. Nailock walked over to him and spoke. "Sire, we have a foothold on each island. Your regular forces could secure them. But Mylako, I fear, will not fall easily."

"You fear! You fear! Ha! They will fall just like the rest of the kingdoms," Malechar spoke harshly. "The others talked bravely, and yet with little force did I subdue them." He turned to Nailock and held his fist level to his face. "Force!" he shouted. "This world fears my force and falls before it. Mylako will fall just as easily, and they will beg me to rule them benevolently just as this continent did." And with this, Malechar laughed contemptuously.

"You are surely great, my lord Malechar," Nailock responded. "But the reports from the royal families are that king Bathen will not fold."

"That old fool," Malechar cried. "He will fold and beg for mercy. And to show the people my will, I will kill him before them. Once done, the islands will tremble at my feet."

"King Bathen will not lead them, my lord," Nailock answered. "They will be led by a man called Booter. He is their captain. Many here say he will not fear death to fight for his islands. These are a strange people, my lord. Perhaps we should have your regular army join your bodyguard, also, just to be safe."

"Safe!" Malechar screamed. "Our forces will be equal in number. With my power, each man will equal many. Perhaps you should stay here on the continent where you will be safe."

With that demeaning remark ringing in his ear, Nailock stepped back, then he spoke. "I will fight with the guard, my lord. But I thought just this once you might stay here until the first battle. I am only concerned for you."

"Concern yourself no more," Malechar seethed. Grabbing Nailock by the throat, he spoke again. "Speak no more on this, Nailock, or I will put my sword through you." Then he tossed the gasping man backward several paces into a wooden table. "No one will be able to stand before me. As long as I lead the guard, they will be invincible."

Nailock lay gasping on the floor. He also recalled the stories of Anasha and his power, but now he feared to question Malechar on such a matter.

The people of the continent were indeed subdued. Everyone despised Malechar, but they feared his power. Thousands had died for no other reason than for Malechar to show the people his absolute control over them. Never before had such brutality been displayed. The old conduct of war had been cast asunder, as soldier and civilian alike were fair game for such horrible conduct done by such horrible warriors. The continent's only hope was the island of Eden and king Bathen. But even this hope was small and grew less as Malechar's forces were gathered to invade Eden. They knew first hand the awful power of this man and the evil of his bodyguard.

They quickly quelled any uprising. And it was common for them, after subjugating those involved, to loot and plunder the area. Very few captives were taken except to be personal slaves of the guard. These poor souls lived for a short time only, and the pain and misery inflicted upon them usually caused their deaths. By such means were the people enslaved. Most fearsome of all was Shebanja.

He was the lieutenant in Malechar's bodyguard, taking orders only from Malechar and Nailock. Were it not for Nailock's strategic mastery, Shebanja would be in command of the guard. His vicious ways were notorious amongst even his own men, and Malechar let him have free reign over his terrifying actions. Both men knew how terror could easily vanquish an enemy as well as cold hard steel of the sword and lance. Both men enjoyed the reaction of their enemy to such tactics. Only Malechar exceeded Shebanja in the use of terror.

Malechar stood before the guard as they gathered in formation. They were ten thousand strong, and there was no mistaken this force but to be an elite unit. They were dressed in leather pants and shirts with a short tunic draped about the shoulders. This covering was dyed black for camouflage at night and for the frightening effect it gave to their enemy. The only part of their clothing not black was their arms, covered by chain mail burnished dark to add to the effect.

This unit was Malechar's military strength, and as named, his bodyguard. There was no fraternization by them with any part of the army, nor did they mingle with the citizenry. Their features were colorless, humorless, and their eyes seemed always to be looking past one, as though looking with a faraway glare.

It was reported that only they were given a special drink prepared daily by one man who mixed it with certain drugs ordered by Malechar. When battle was to take place, a more powerful dose was given to each. It produced a drone-like hive of men. But make no mistake about it, it was an efficient unit of men, uncaring in anything but to obey their master, to kill and to die for him. Their purpose was one, and their will and strength became superhuman in their resolve for him.

Such an army was now standing before Malechar, and he seemed pleased. "Tomorrow as day breaks we leave these shores," Malechar screamed as he raised his arms. "Tomorrow you will stand before your conquered foe, and you will rule the world."

They returned his shout with yells while banging their swords against their shields. To those who stood near and watched, chills came upon them, and they wondered who could stand before such a man who led such an army.

Malechar bid Nailock and Shebanji towards him. After they approached and bowed, he spoke. "Nailock, you will ride in the rear boat in the fleet to make sure that we will approach the shore almost as one. We must make our landing quickly for that may be our only weakness."

"But, my lord, should I not be next to you to shield whatever the enemy cast your way?" Nailock asked, knowing that this was a demeaning gesture by Malechar.

"Do as you are told," he spoke. "Shebanja, you will ride next to me and on my command lead the men to fight."

"Yes, my lord," Shebanja replied, looking sneeringly at Nailock. At last, he was second in command. He would prove to his master that he, Shabanja, was most deserving.

"In this one thing, Shebanja, do not fail," Malechar said slowly, deeply, and threateningly. "Do not, repeat, do not harm the royal family. Their death must come after the battle."

"May I ask why, my lord?" Shebanja questioned. "They are the enemy, are they not?"

"I said so," Malechar shouted. "You could not understand." He looked far away and stared for several moments. "It is written thusly, that is the way they must perish," he almost whispered, and then continued. "You will recognize them by their uniforms. Their soldiers will wear a blue top with a white cross in front. The royal family will have five stars in the right upper corner."

Malechar looked sharply at Shebanja, and his eyes glowed sharply as he talked. "Remember this, Shebanja, and make sure every man knows it, too. A slow and agonizing death awaits those who forgets this." Few things ever frightened Shebanja, but that icy glow from Malechar's eyes brought a shiver to him and fear seized him in that instant.

Nailock stood for a moment in place as Malechar and Shebanja walked away together. Then quickly, he marched to join them as they entered the building. Malechar asked Shebanja what he wanted, and he replied. "Sire, there is talk about a great sorcerer on the island. Will he cause trouble?"

Malechar picked up an iron rod and banged it against an oval ring producing a loud ringing clang. In seconds, there appeared a servant bowing to the evil lord. "Bring me Sophia, the prophetess."

"Not even Anasha can foresee as this woman is able to, and her skill further enhances my power." Malechar smiled an evil smile and looked towards his two lieutenants. "She comes to me by way of the eastern Blackroth principality. She foretold of our coming, but those poor fools did not believe her or use her skills. Ha! They didn't even know what power she possesses. And now I can plan any battle for victory because I know what my enemies will do beforehand."

"But what if she is wrong?" Nailock questioned.

"Sophia is never wrong. NEVER!" Malechar bellowed "Before you ask, I keep her younger brother alive and locked safely away so that she can not refuse me. He is the only member of the family left alive after I conquered her land and people. To enslave her, I murdered her mother and sisters before her eyes. She knows I will not hesitate to torture her brother before her either. She fears this more than anyone fears death." Slamming his fist into the table, he cried sternly. "This is how to rule. Fear. Find out the fear one has and you have won and enslaved."

The door swung open and in walked the servant pulling on a thin chain that was attached to the neck of Sophia, the prophetess. Nailock and Shebanja bowed slightly, and even Malechar nodded his head in acknowledgment, such was her beauty and bearing. She was tall and willowy, and the dark dress of black leather made her appear even taller. Her face was of the fairest complexion and unblemished. Her eyes were deep blue, penetrating in their stare but sad in their countenance.

"What does my lord desire?" She spoke so softly that no one made a sound so as to hear her every word.

"Sophia," Malechar replied as softly, and he pointed to a chair for her to sit down. As she seated herself, he continued. "I will not keep you too long for I know how draining your powers are to you. Tell us, when we land on the main island of Mylako, how will the battle proceed?"

There was silence as Sophia closed her eyes and took several deep breaths and then seemingly appeared to stop breathing. Nailock shifted uneasily after several long moments and was about to speak, but was stopped by Malechar, who without taking his eyes off Sophia, waved his hand to stop any such words. Her eyes opened wide and she spoke. "They will meet you very near the shore, my lord, prepared to do battle."

Malechar just stared at the prophetess for several moments as if in disbelief, and then he slammed his fist together. "They will meet us near the shore to do battle? Such insolence!"

He walked around the table with quickened steps. He then stopped abruptly and spoke again before either Nailock or Shebanja could speak. "They are going to let us land uncontested with perhaps many times their number and yet will do battle against us?"

"We will surely cut them to bits and be quickly done with them," Shebanja cried out. "They must be a stupid people to want to face us head on."

"By the gods," Malechar boomed. "What a marvelous race we will encounter. What a brave people to want to die in such manner. All the nations in this continent sued for peace and quickly cowered before us."

Turning again to Sophia, Malechar questioned. "What do you see ... how will the battle go?"

Without hesitation, Sophia replied. "There will be great carnage, annihilation, and total conquest such as never witnessed before, my lord Malechar."

"Splendid!" Malechar cried. "My soldiers hunger for battle and for blood."

"There will be much blood, my lord" The prophetess spoke eagerly. Nailock looked quizzically at Sophia, for this was the first time she spoke without being asked. Her tone was slightly different, and yet ... He wanted to bring this up to Malechar, but thought better than to break the gleeful mood his master now beheld, for such moods were rarely seen by him.

"You have answered well, Sophia," Malechar spoke. "Go back to your room. You are dismissed."

"Will not Anasha have equal power to foresee our moves, sire? What if he counters what the prophetess has foreseen?" Shebanja questioned, but then he bowed slightly at his impertinence.

"Put your concern away. Sophia is never wrong. This is one distinction that only I believe in. Still, I marvel at their ignorance about her that those fools held while they had her. And now they are our slaves, as well the kingdom of Mylako shall be."

"But what of Anasha?"

"Forget the old fool for now."

In the main castle of the land of Blackroth, a door opens to the prisoner's room. A man well worn in years of service enters carrying a tray of food. Sensing no one was listening, he spoke. "It is I, Springer, sir. Malechar plans to attack the island with his bodyguard, and after securing the island complex, he plans to return here."

"Here?" Prince Asher asked. "Why would he come back so soon? What are his plans, friend?"

"He is here to return, and then both of you will go back to Froth."

"Do you know why he wants to go back to Froth, sir?" Singer replied. "I heard that Malechar needs to return for either orders from his lord or a renewal of his strengths."

Asher looked at him quizzically. "I don't understand."

"Our sources did not get the opportunity to learn either, sir. We lost two men already who ventured into Froth. That is, we never heard from them again. However, we do know there is a source that gives him his power," replied Springer.

"Tell me, sir," Asher asked as he put his arm over the man's shoulder. "How long have you worked for my father, or should I say Anasha?"

"A long time, my prince. Now I will only say those of us here loyal to Eden work for both men. We have been communicating with them almost everyday through the use of birds. A most splendid idea of Anasha, I must say. We have sent word to your father of your condition, sire. He knows you are now safe but imprisoned."

"My son!" Asher asked. "Is my wife and son safe?"

"For now, my lord, Anasha has your son at his place in the forest. Even should Malechar prevail, to find where they could hide would take his entire army."

"I miss them so," Asher spoke, and he held his head in his hands. "What are our chances for success, Springer? After all, Captain Booter holds the reins of the army now. He is an able man. Tell me now, I want your honest reply."

"Even Captain Booter won't be able to stand against Malechar."

Prince Asher looked harshly at the servant. "I am sorry, sir," spoke Springer. "I am afraid what I speak is true." Kneeling before the prince, he spoke again. "My lord, by tomorrow, you may be the only royal member alive, except for your son, who will have to flee indefinitely."

Prince Asher looked at the man with compassion now. He had risked his life to be here, and sadly, Asher knew the truth had been spoken. Lifting the faithful servant to his feet, Asher guided him to the door. "Send word to my father that I still live. Let him know all you told me. God speed to you," spoke Asher.

Squeezing the prince's hand, Springer left the room and disappeared into the hallway. Prince Asher gloomily sat down and thought of all that was said. Sobs soon came from him as he feared for his family and for his beloved Eden.

SCROLL V

The messenger hurriedly brought the carrier bird over to the court where king Bathen and his retinue sat. The capsule was removed from the bird's leg, and the message was delicately removed and unwound. "Call Captain Booter in here immediately," the king commanded. From the room where he was going over the preparations of war, Booter quickly entered into the chamber.

Captain Booter took the note that the king handed him and squinted his eyes to read the very fine print. "Your son still lives and is well," he read aloud. The king sat down next to princess Sara and patted her arm. Shouts of joy were uttered from everyone as they heard the news, knowing how welcomed it would be for the royal family.

But the king could see that Booter was still reading on, and he quieted the room. "Read on, Captain," the king beckoned.

"Sire! I am afraid the rest is what we feared equally as much as harm to the prince," Booter replied. "The invasion force of Malechar leaves tomorrow at dawn. Miraculously, we also know where he will land."

Stunned by the news each had been expecting, everyone stood for several minutes, mute and not moving. The king dismissed them and stood alone with Captain Booter.

"This is news we expected at any time, and yet I do not know how to accept it," the king spoke slowly. "Even as a young man, Captain, I never could get use to the fear of battle."

"Nor I, your majesty," answered Booter. "But you always performed courageously and honorably. Your feats were an inspiration to those of us trained for the military."

"Thank you for such kind words, my friend. But now we must fight a battle that I had hoped never to fight. The very existence of our kingdom depends on the outcome of the battle tomorrow." Wearily, the king poured himself a goblet of wine and continued. "The light of freedom has gone out on the mainland, and for those tortured souls over there, we are their last hope. We are fighting a man who knows no chivalry in his manner, no charity in his heart. We will be fighting an army driven by evil and maintained by evil."

"I will call all the officers into the war room," Captain Booter spoke. "Go freshen up, my lord. We will wait for you there and prepare our line of defense."

The king nodded his approval and Booter left the room. He then rang the bell for a servant. Quickly, he took a quill and paper and began writing. After several minutes, he rolled the paper up and sealed it. In moments a horseman was on his way towards Anasha. There was too much to say, and now too little time to say it.

It was midday as the officers of Eden gathered about their king. There were ten lieutenants under Captain Booter. Each one commanded approximately one thousand men. Normally, the five islands were maintained by a regular army of one thousand men. But now the pending war had marshaled all able bodied men of the islands. It was mandatory to serve five years in military training from the age of sixteen to twenty one, so the men now called upon were not novices to the use of weapons or tactics of battle.

This was not the same kind of army that had gathered before Malechar. They were gathered together by patriotism, not hate. They were drawn together by necessity, not for evil destruction. But Malechar's guard had been battle tested for the last several months, and Eden's army awaited their trial by blood. The only common denominator was that each was willing to die for their cause and for their leader.

King Bathen entered the room and sat in the main chair overlooking the table where maps and papers lay exposed before him. Around the table sat the officers in strict attention. Immediately, Captain Booter addressed him. "Sire, for the last several days we have been going over several battle plans. Now that we know where Malechar will land, we have our plans narrowed down to two. I will present these two to you, and you make the final decision."

The king knew Captain Booter had been going over plans for battle for many days with all the officers, including himself. Scores of places where Malechar could land were exposed and strategies discussed. Every officer was given his opportunity to speak. In fact, each one was prodded into decision when no one came freely. Nodding, he allowed Booter to continue.

"Here is where he will land, my lord." Booter spoke and pointed to the area on the map. "The area, as you know, is fairly wide open and flat so his crafts will have no trouble. It is the area we ourselves had figured was best to invade us. One plan is to have a massive attack by bow and arrow on the army as it attempts to land. We may be able to create many casualties this way. Once they do land, then we will attack them on the beach and our one and only stand will be made here. Half the officers here feel this is the plan we should commit ourselves to."

He hesitated at this time to let the king think on this plan. Hearing no questions, he continued. "The other plan is to allow the army to land unmolested. They will advance several hundred meters inward to this plane of open land where we will be waiting. Seeing us, they will form their force into a cavalry positioned ready to attack. We will then meet them head on with our own charge. Here we will hold back about a fifth of our men so we will be outnumbered. However, our object will be to meet them with this one thrust and to inflict as many casualties as possible. We will then immediately withdraw and flee into the forest. I am sure Malechar and his guard will pursue, thinking we have been so weakened by our charge. Awaiting them will be two thousand archers who will rain down a torrent of arrows upon them as to cause great confusion until we can reorganize. The remaining warfare will be conducted throughout the forest in hit and run tactics. The forest will be our provider, but to Malechar it will be a curse. It is this plan that the other half favors."

After several moments, the king spoke. "What do you favor, Mr. Booter?"

"Frankly, sire," he answered. "There is much to be said about attacking them as they try to land. However, I feel this exposes our entire force, plus I don't think they are aware of our force of archers. I favor the second plan. After all, the forest has always been a part of us, and now it will be our greatest ally. It will take away their use of lancers and limit the use of swords. Our strength will then be in the ability to hit them fast and hard with arrows. Hopefully, to wear them down to where we can then hunt them in small groups."

"It does seem to be a very good plan," the king mentioned. "However, could we not combine part of the first with the second? I do like the idea of firing a cloud of arrows into their ranks as they still try to land."

"Perhaps, my king," Captain Booter replied. "But we should not try to deviate now from one plan or the other. To do so, weakens one plan more so than it does to strengthen the other."

"You are probably correct, as usual, Mr. Booter," the king said. "Come, come, gentlemen. Do you have any exceptions or objections? Say so now or hold your peace. Once we agree, we will do it. I found out it is better to make a decision and stick to it than not have one at all and then make changes as we go."

"Sire!" cried out lieutenant Greenlee. "I understand these warriors are different than any army ever known. That not only will a nonfatal wound not stop them, but sometimes a fatal wound will not stop them for some time. I have heard reports that some of them fought with arrows pierced through their chest and swords buried into their midsections."

There was a pause of several moments before the king spoke. "I understand your concern and fear, gentlemen. I can not hold back any truth from you, nor do I expect you to hold back any from your men. This is an evil force we are going to fight. What kind of spell they are under, or how to break it has not come to us yet. But fight on, my brave men. Our islands and our families depend upon how well we fight."

The lieutenant sat down, and he cast his eyes downward half ashamed to have admitted his fear. The king stood up and circled the table, placing his hand upon the young man's shoulder. "To face the enemy in battle is always a terrifying experience. One never knows if he will live or die or if he will perform admirably at all. Your worries are genuine, and so do I know is your patriotism. None of us here may be alive after tomorrow, but what is much more important is that we will have done our duty. I have no fear that you will not. I send you into battle with a very heavy heart for your responsibility is great and your chances slim. May God be with us." And saying this, king Bathen gently squeezed upon the lieutenant.

"God be with us," spoke the officers in chorus. "And God save the king."

"As the king mentioned, we don't know what gives Malechar's bodyguard its strength or its ability to withstand various wounds that would normally cripple or kill." Captain Booter pointed to where the invasion was to take place on the map and continued. "One of the main reasons for the battle plan we chose is, hopefully, Malechar's men will become worn down as they chase us through our beloved forest. We hope to sap them of their strength, to make them mortal men, to make them susceptible to our steel."

All eyes scanned the maps upon the table. No one spoke for all was said in the days proceeding, and now all the preparation was concluded.

But all the planning and guessing could not call upon death to share its mystery. Only on the battlefield would each man know if death would point its macabre finger and say "come."

"Gentlemen!" Captain Booter spoke loud and clear. "If there are no further questions, go to your units and see to it that all is prepared. We will all meet at the assigned stations near the beach at daybreak." Hearing no other comments, he dismissed them and sat along with the king.

"War is for the young, Mr. Booter," sighed Bathen. "In my youth, the clash of swords and the thundering of horses excited and thrilled me. Now, I am sickened to send these young warriors to what, in all probability, will be their deaths. The young may desire it, but the elderly must make the decisions. What tomorrows can we give them?"

"Don't be so hard on yourself, sire," Captain Booter replied. "We have no choice now but to fight. Most have never seen battle. I only hope we stand and fight well."

"Still! I often wonder that maybe we should reverse our techniques. Why send our best and our young to the slaughter. Let them have their tomorrows, and in their twilight years, send the old to battle. I am sure that would end many a desire for conflict." He laughed low to himself. "Not a bad idea, eh Mr. Booter?"

"Rest now, my lord," Booter requested. "Go to your princess and solace her. Her calamity must be greater than ours for we can fight while she must sit and wait, as all our women must do. I am going to Mary now. So much to say and no time to say it."

Bending low to his king, he then straightened and left. And the king sat and reflected on his youth, on his son, on his grandson. He wanted to think of anything but not of tomorrow.

SCROLL VI

A ndrew thought he heard a twig snap by the tree. Cautiously, he approached it in a wide arc with his sword drawn. "Step forth!" He cried out. "Prepare to meet your doom. I have come to claim this forest and all the inhabitants therein."

"Never will you have Eden or any of our lands," responded the voice behind the shield. Quickly, two wooden swords clashed, as prince Abrams jumped out from behind the tree. "I will defeat thee, lord Malechar." The battle raged on for several minutes with no quarter given by either contestant. But then Andrew tripped over a log and exposed himself to Abram's sword. The prince put it to Andrew's heart and pretended to thrust, and the battle was over.

They laughed for a long time at the outcome. Each had taken turns hunting the other down in the woods, and throughout the day had enjoyed the play of war. Exhausted for the time being, they lay upon the forest floor and talked. How many times over their short lifetime had they played the games of young boys could not be counted. If each had been the other's brother, their love for one another could not have been greater.

"Boy, am I hungry," spoke Abrams. "I could eat a horse."

"Two horses and a cow," said Andrew, and they laughed even harder.

After they quieted down, Andrew again spoke. "Has Anasha ever found a way to really defeat Malechar? My father said he is driven by a force that even Anasha may not be able to defeat."

"I have seen the look on grandfather's face when I asked him how he would defeat Malechar," answered the prince. "He seemed like he was far away in thought."

"I am frightened, Abrams," replied Andrew. Turning his head to stifle his tears, he continued. "I am not sure I will see my father again, nor my mother and sisters. Father told me to be brave and to do my duty, and yet, how can he do his against Malechar?"

"What is his duty?" questioned the prince.

"To fight Malechar's army," said Andrew.

"If he fights Malechar but doesn't defeat him, did he still do his duty?"

"Why, yes!" exclaimed Andrew. "He did not say he had to defeat him but only to fight him." After several moments of thought, he again spoke. "I get a funny feeling inside thinking about not seeing my father. Do you feel the same about yours?"

"I miss him very much." said the prince in a soft voice. "I do not know if he is dead or not from day to day. I try not to cry, but at night I can not help it."

"I wish we were old enough to fight for our country," Andrew spoke, and he swung his sword at an imaginary target. "What did Anasha say to you last night when you talked with him?"

Anasha say to you last night when you talked with him?""He spoke strangely to me, Andrew. He said that if someone pure in heart or noble in deed came forth, someone who was the opposite of Malechar's evil, then perhaps he could be defeated. He read about an ancient legend of our country where golden swords were used to thwart a terrible enemy. Those swords gave our ancestors a strange power by which they overcame the enemy."

"Where could we find such swords?" Andrew excitedly asked. "Do our fathers know of such weapons?"

"I asked Anasha the same question," Abrams replied. "He said it was only a very old story in one of his very old scrolls. Although he confessed that which he reads was once true, but he himself does not know where such weapons would be stored."

They heard the swift pounding of a horse's hooves heading towards the cottage. They both jumped up and ran to hear the news the rider carried. When they came to the opening of the lot, they could see the messenger talking to Anasha standing in the doorway. Anasha then put his arm around the man and bid him to enter.

Anasha looked at the boys with weary eyes as they entered the main room. "Tomorrow the battle begins," he said. "Gather your belongings so that we may be prepared to flee. You will be, I am afraid, a very good prize for Malechar, my little prince."

"Surely you don't think our army will fold without a fight," prince Abrams harshly spoke. "I would like to think the battle will last more than just one day."

"Quiet down, my prince," Anasha spoke as he motioned with his hand to silence the prince. "Our warriors are very worthy. However, my job is to be rational. I must tell you honestly that never before have our islands been in such grave danger. The army your grandfather, and your father, Andrew, fights is not ordinary." He shuffled over to his paper on another table and continued. "Your experience is very limited. But there are many different kinds of people in this world." Sternly, he looked at them. "There are many different forces in this world, too. Unfortunately for all of us, a very evil one is on the move, and I am equally afraid it is a dominating one."

"Have we no recourse, Anasha?" Abrams loudly spoke.

"All things come and go and come again," Anasha replied softly. "We can only do the best we can do while we are here."

The messenger was eating now, more gulping down his food than chewing it. Anasha told him that after a short rest to hurry back to join his forces and to let the king know that the prince was in good care. Just as they had planned, he, Anasha would do.

The two boys stepped outside, and Abrams spoke. "There is just enough light to get back tonight. I am going to follow the messenger back. Anasha will be furious so let him think I am here with you."

"We can't do that," Andrew answered. "We are suppose to stay here."

"Our country needs every able warrior now," Abrams replied. "It is time I swing a real sword. I will not run away day by day forever. My duty is with my king."

"My duty is to be with you," Andrew boldly spoke. "My pledge to my father was to protect you, and I will not break this pledge."

They grasp hands and hurried to saddle their horses. While the young prince walked them to the edge of the forest to await the messenger, Andrew went into the kitchen area and stuffed bread and meat into his shirt. As inconspicuously as he could, he ambled out to meet with his friend. They tore at the bread and meat in their hunger.

Minutes later, they saw the messenger mount his horse and soon he was galloping past them. Letting him get about one hundred meters ahead, they then followed him. They laughed at their triumph, knowing Anasha would not miss them until darkness.

The pace was much swifter than they imagined, for if darkness descended before they left the forest, they would have to wait until dawn. In the dark of the woods, travel was impossible, so rapidly the messenger drove his steed unknowingly dragging the boys in frightful pursuit. Tenaciously, the rider was followed until the forest's edge was reached. Gratefully, they rode from it as the last rays of the sun penetrated the solid green wall.

They watched as the rider entered the courtyard. It was not guarded because of the encampment along the perimeter away from the forest side. In minutes, night came to embrace the island and only the glow of the campfires in the camp and the torches and lanterns in the castle gave light.

It was easy to walk about without being seen. Carefully, they made their way into the room next to the kitchen. Only a servant was in there. What seemed as a long time to the boys finally passed before the servant left. Quietly they loaded themselves down with food, and grabbing a pitcher of water, they walked out. After several minutes of carefully avoiding a servant here and there, they made their way to the stables. Climbing a ladder to a loft, they set the food before them and ate.

Quietly, Andrew spoke to the prince. "Abrams, what do you plan to do in the morning?"

"There should be no one in the guardhouse come morning. There, the uniforms are kept for the guards. At the end of the room, there is a large chest. In it is my uniform. Also, there will be my shield and sword."

"Why is everything kept there and not in your room?" Andrew asked. "By the way, what can I wear?"

"You can wear one of the guard's uniforms," Abrams answered. "There are always extras. As for mine being there, quite simply, mother said there was no room for them in my room."

Andrew reached out his hand. Prince Abrams took hold of it. "Tomorrow we shall defend our kingdom," spoke Andrew. "Whatever happens, you are my dear friend, Abrams."

"You are mine, too," Abrams replied. "We shall fight together and our families will be so proud."

For several minutes they lay silent, both were looking out on the starry night through the loft window. It was difficult to envision the camp of war nearby while this peaceful canopy hovered over them. Weariness enveloped them, and soon Abrams heard his dear friend in deep sleep. He, himself, felt the tiredness of his body succumbing to the sweet sensation of sleep. Sleep well, my friend, he thought. Do not hate me for what I will do in the morning, but I will not let you fight and die tomorrow. Perhaps your time will come when I am long gone, but tomorrow's responsibility will be mine and mine alone. Then he drifted into nothingness.

The crow of the cock awakened them. After stretching and yawning themselves awake, they snickered and then chuckled at each other as they relieved themselves in the corner of the loft. Hearing a noise below, they quietly sat upon the hay. It was a servant throwing hay to the few horses that had been left behind, and in minutes he was gone. Unwrapping the left over bread and meat, both boys ate sparingly and slowly. Now, not much was said as they looked at one another. Not having much appetite, soon they slowly and carefully climbed down the ladder of the loft. Andrew went first and with a couple of steps left, he jumped down and waited as Abrams started his descent.

Upon reaching the floor, both looked about to make sure no one was in the area. The blow to the head was sudden, terribly frightening to the assaulter. Never had either one hit the other except in play with no intent to hurt. Now, trembling hands checked the pulse and the breath of the other.

Relieved to see that the hit did the job, quickly rope and gag was applied. Dragging the limp body to a corner, hay was thrown over it to cover any clothing. Then looking about and seeing no one, he scrambled to the guardhouse only meters away.

How handsome he looked in uniform with its white cross and stars on the blue background. What a fine warrior prince I'll be today he thought as he swung the sword about the room. The sun upon its silver blade made the heart quicken. Carefully, he retraced his steps back to the stable to retrieve a horse.

All together, a couple hours has passed since daybreak. It would take another hour or so to slowly slip into the forest and work along its edge to the battle area. If everything Anasha said was going to happen as planned, it would take only a short wait then before the enemy arrived. Patting the horse in its neck, he slowly rode to the forest.

SCROLL VII

King Bathen rode slowly through the encampment of his army. Now his figure appeared majestic as he sat straight and proud. Even if he was without his jeweled helmet and the uniform of the royal house, one could tell of his royal bearing. He returned the greetings of his men as they gestured. His eyes scanned them all, watching them sharpening their blades and swinging their swords. It was a grand army led by a grand king.

"My lord!" Captain Booter's voice cried out. "All is ready." As he rode up to meet the king, he continued. "The men have eaten and seem to be in fine spirits."

"Yes, yes," the king replied. "It is a fine day to do battle." He stopped his mount and gazed over the area. "You know, this will be the only time I have ever led my army to battle on our own soil. I did a bit of fighting as a young man, but it was always on the continent. I am not one for superstition or such, but I do pray this is not a foreboding. My father use to tell me when an army fights on its own soil, it is usually fighting for its life."

"We are fighting for our lives, sire. But with God's good grace, we shall overcome and be victorious." And Captain Booter rode forward pointing his sword towards the sea. "We will make our stand there, your majesty. We will let Malechar land unmolested to gauge his strength. If our reports are right, we should be equal in number overall. We will attack in equal ranks from both sides so as to hide the fact that our archers lie in waiting." He hesitated, them continued. "Should we falter, then we will retreat back here in the forest where our diversionary action will be to attack the enemy with hit and run tactics."

"It is probably the best plan, Captain," spoke the king. "It may gain us the time we need to deplete Malechar's strength, and to weaken his men through hunger and fatigue. However, because we may be equal in number does not mean we will be equal in strength. My last talk with Anasha was only of bitter news. This army we face is driven be evil, and as we will grow weaker, it will grow stronger, nourished by the fear and blood it creates."

"I have not told anyone of this, sire," Booter replied. "Does the king wish it so?"

"No, no!" Bathen whispered. "You did right. They know their cause is just, let them fight with that on their minds."

They watched as the men continued their preparations. Finally, the king spoke. "How is your wife, Mary? It is always so hard on the wives. I saw Sara last night. We talked for a long time, about everything but this battle. She is a good women... reminds me of my queen, God rest her soul."

"Aye, lord." Booter answered. "Mary has always been so understanding. But this war is different, and she senses it. I need not say it, but she is glad Andrew is with prince Abarms. Better they are both with Anasha. That sly fox will keep Malechar searching forever in these woods."

"Ah! Yes, the forest." Bathen laughed. "It is our source of strength and being. Anasha will keep the wolves at bay all right. I miss the old devil already. He is like these woods ... old, wise, and secretive."

"My lord," Captain Booter asked, almost hesitantly. "Where does this man, Malechar, and his army get their strength? If we knew that, then perhaps, perhaps we could find a way to deplete it. I am not afraid of battle. But this ... this is not war. If what you say is true, then we are sheep to the slaughter."

The king gazed at his chief officer, hard at first, then softly. He placed his hand upon the captain's shoulder, but Booter continued. "Forgive me, my king. I do not fear death, and my life belongs to the royal house. These men of ours are simple men, yet they are now so brave and noble. I will follow you anywhere, and they will follow me. Are we fighting shadows? Where will our honor be this day? Sire! After hopeless bloodshed, the royal families of each state on the continent capitulated, and yet they outnumbered this tyrant, this mutant."

He then let his mount carry him a few steps away from the king. "I am ashamed to say this, my lord. But is this a battle that is going to be worth fighting? Will not the same results be what will be if we do not fight?"

Again, the king moved to Captain Booter and touched him. "From any other man I would deem those words treason. There must be great ache in your heart and turmoil in your soul. Your thoughts are my thoughts, my dear captain. There was no sleep for me last night, nor for the last several nights. If what you say is true, then death will be in vain. Believe me, should Malechar ask for my head to appease him and his killing, I will give it."

Captain Booter looked aghast, but Bathen put his finger to his own lips to silence him. "There will be no sacrifice. I have lived long, and amongst the things I have learned are that such men as Malechar will not be appeased by peaceful coexistence, nor will they ask for such. He will want only supreme control and total obedience. I will die this day, as will most of this army. What saddens me is that he will want my family to die, too. Such is the way that such men live and that such men think. The land and people he conquers will know no charity nor benevolence."

"If we must fight and die, that is our duty," Captain Booter cut in. "Why would he want to kill the remaining members of your family. After all, he spared the royal families abroad. Surely, he will spare yours."

"You asked earlier if Malechar's strength could be weakened. I do not know how, but there is always hope. But whence he came, the land of Froth, there is where his strength lies. He is a prince himself, you know. In fact, his family and ours are kinsman."

"What!" Booter exclaimed. "You say you are related to this monster, and yet he wages war on us. Then you say he will exterminate your house. Sire, I am afraid I am lost by all this. Why did you not tell me sooner?"

"There is so much to tell, and yet there isn't. But our relationship dooms me and my family. There were several marriages between the families when all was in harmony. Then, generations ago our families quarreled violently. The particulars escape now, at least their importance does. But we fought and our side won and banished them into what was considered a forbidden area on the continent. It is considered that way now so you can imagine how it must have been then. The head of their family was a prince called Adofus, who vowed he would come back to drive us into submission and to eliminate our royal seed. What seemed like idle threats then now seem to be coming true."

"After all these years such hate lives," Booter remarked. "How can they hate you for something that happened so long ago?"

"I will not go into length now. In fact, you would never know were it not for this war, captain. But they, like us, had a royal sorcerer by the name of Canasish, a most wicked man. According to Anasha, it is he that keeps the hate alive, the quest for vengeance alive."

The king studies Booter's expression and then continued. "Yes! Anasha believes he still lives after all these years. We are talking centuries perhaps. You are a soldier, captain, and the best I've seen at your business. But I am a king, privy to knowledge from people like Anasha, and old books that you are not aware of nor allowed to know. But believe me, such things can happen, as strange as they seem."

"But, but we are saying a man has been alive for several lifetimes. Sire, I can't believe that."

"It does not matter now what you believe, captain. I am telling you this now because I believe you'll be dead this day, as I will... that is what I believe. Whatever power over life Canasish has discovered, whatever strength he gave Malechar is hidden from us now, Anasha knows of Canasish and he of him. Anasha's family has given us wisdom and knowledge of our entire existence. It was his ancestry that helped defeat Adofus, and believe me Anasha is as doomed as we are. Anasha is good, and such goodness can not exist with Canasish. He will have Anasha hunted down until caught."

"After so many years, and there never has been an attempt at reconciliation?"

"Yes, we have tried. After many years when the exile was imposed, we sent emissaries to Froth. The first came back alive but blinded. The others had only their heads sent back. After a while, no one seen entering Froth was ever seen returning. Malechar was the first to ever come out of Froth. My God! Such pent up hate. Such dangerous hate to have waited this long until it became invincible."

"My lord, are there no reports from our people on the continent that speaks comfort for us?"

"None. However, it has been overheard that once Malechar conquers us, he must return to Froth. Whether it is to be rejuvenated or to bring back Canasish in triumph, no one knows."

A trumpet sounded loudly, even though it was in the distance. Malechar's armada had been sighted and activity from Eden's army intensified.

"Let every man do his duty, Captain Booter," the king shouted. "We are the only light left in this darkening hour to the good people of the continent. Should we be snuffed out will be left to fate. But in our hand is our destiny as to how well we fight. Let the people know Eden fought with honor and with violence."

The king watched his army move about, first in random movement, then settling into a disciplined manner. He was proud of these men as he saw them take their positions. They gathered about three hundred meters from shore along a wide plain area. Ten thousand warriors were awaiting the command to strike the enemy, to defend their homeland. He watched in inspired awe and pride.

To the left were two thousand of the men on horseback, and to the right another equal number. In the center stood the foot soldier armed with lance and sword. But each warrior was trained in the use of the bow and arrow. Should the attack falter from all three positions, they were to retreat back to the edge of the forest where these weapons awaited them. This was done under cover of the two thousand men in the center that stayed back to rain arrows upon the enemy. Malechar's army may surpass them in strength and even in skill, but it would be a different matter fighting a moving enemy shooting arrows from the dark of the forest. The forest was their one true strength, perhaps it would be their one salvation.

King Bathen could see the boats approaching, and he guessed that within the hour the battle would commence. He knew his son was alive somewhere on the continent, and he was even glad not to have him here knowing death awaited him this day. His thoughts drifted to Anasha and the boys. It would take more then Malechar's army to hunt them down if they fled from spot to spot within the forest. He remembered the joy his grandson gave him, and what pleasure it was to see him grow into a young man.

It was indeed a strange tale he told Captain Booter, he thought. Many did not believe in magic or the power of the royal sorcerers, but he also knew that many things could not be explained by reality. There was a magical force driving Malechar, evil though it be, it was still magical. What magic did he have to combat it? Anasha did not really say he had anything to counteract this evil force. He did mention something though, about when swords of gold were used to fight swords of evil. But he was still into his ancient scrolls, so a definite reply was never given. Right now anything would be nice, for never had Eden seemed so alone, so vulnerable, so near extinction as a life force as she seemed now. Oh my beloved island, he thought, I mean not to let you down ... for my inadequacy, I shall give my life this day for you.

He heard the men calling him, snapping him back from his thoughts of family and land. They beckoned him back to where they stood, ready to do battle to the greatest menace their world had yet known.

SCROLL VIII

The first craft hit shore and there was no denying who Malechar was as the first group of men and their horses clamored onto dry land. He stood taller than the others, and broader at the shoulders. Across his chest was a deep red cross on the black coat. His horse, a massive stallion, was brought to him quickly, and he mounted it. This was a majestic and inspiring sight he presented to the army of Eden. This caused even their horses to reel and paw as they sensed the coming battle.

Bathen and his men watched as barge after barge struck the beach side by side unloading their deadly cargo. He had to admire this terrible army as they efficiently landed and formed their ranks. The sound of the waves and the snorting of horses was all that was heard, as direction was given by silent command by a couple officers pointing their swords where they wanted the men to go. It was indeed an awesome sight as one hundred barges lined the beach, consuming hundreds of meters of shoreline. Chills went upon the men of Eden as the mighty guard of Malechar gathered together and slowly strode forth.

It was well into morning, with the sun shining brightly upon the two armies as they faced each other. They were just over a hundred meters apart. Malechar, with one man next to him on each side, rode in front, with another man slightly behind him.

"Remember," Malechar spoke to Shebanja. "Drive the men forward. I am sure they will flee into their great forest after the initial charge. If we can get part of our force behind them, we can prevent most of that from happening. The king will have his special markings on, let him be mine. Hawthorne, you circle your force into the foot soldiers between them and their cavalry," as he pointed to his right. "Shebanja, you do the same on the other side, just as we planned. Hopefully, we can cut most of their forces down before any escape."

He chuckled deeply, and Shebanja and Hawthorne joined in, too. "How easy this should be, for no one can match our strength." Turning his head, he spoke to Nailock riding behind him. "While the fighting continues, drive your small band straight ahead to drive through and get behind. Get as close to the forest's edge as you can and then wait. Soon you will have stragglers from Bathen's army fleeing to you. Butcher them, Nailock, and I'll leave you ruler of these islands while I return to Froth."

"But, my lord," cried Shebanja. "Am I not your second in command?"

"Silence!" Hissed Malechar. "Do your duty well, and while I am away you will rule the continent."

Shebanja smiled a wicked smile, and his eyes gleamed at the thought. I will fight like a demon, he thought to himself. You may have the power of Froth, I will be happy with the five states of the continent and all their possessions.

Malechar raised his hand to stop his army. Then he rode forward a few steps. Shouting so all in Eden's army could hear, he spoke. "Hear me soldiers of Eden. Lay down your arms, and bring your king to me, and I will spare you your lives. Do this and live, or fight and each one of you will die."

He waited several moments to let the words sink in, then shouted again. "Let us retire from this place, and you, all of you can go home to wives and family. Just bring me your king before me and you may live."

The horses pawed nervously at the ground as each rider fidgeted in his saddle and each foot soldier moved slightly about his spot.

The king looked about his men, and then spoke to Captain Booter. "Perhaps I was wrong, Captain. It may be best for me to give myself up so that the men will have a chance. The other way is surely death."

Captain Booter seized Bathen's reins. "No, my lord. I was wrong. I almost tremble at this man's army, but I would rather die than have his foot upon my neck and to enslave all of Eden. You will stay here and lead us to battle. You have led us all our lives, now lead us today."

As these words were spoken, a single rider was seen galloping out of the forest towards Malechar. It was hard to make him out at first, then a horrified look came over the king's face. "My God!" he shouted. "It's prince Abrams. My boy, my beloved grandson, what is he doing here?" Transfixed, the men of Eden watched the boy ride up to the enemy. Silently, yet frozen in place, to hear what might transpire, they strained their senses.

The shrill voice of the boy came through his helmet loud enough for both armies to hear. "You have transgressed upon our land to subdue us and to cause great harm. Therefore, you are Eden's enemy and mine. Leave this island or suffer our might and our will. You can not conquer us as you did the others, for this is Eden." And he slowly drew his sword and held it high, as it shined bright silver in the sky.

Malechar cocked his head and listened in wonder at such bravery and audacity. Truly, he thought, this is indeed a different and marvelous people. Perhaps such an enemy could even earn his respect.

"Swine!" Shenbanja screamed. "No puny boy will stand in our way, nor shout false words to this army and to lord Malechar." And he unsheathed his sword and with lightning swiftness swung it.

It all seemed in slow motion to Malechar as the horror of what was happening unfolded. Quickly, he reached to subdue Shebanja's swing but was not fast enough. The blade slashed through the boy's neck, and the head tumbled sideways with his blood spurting violently forth. It seemed as though he was frozen in time, with his hand and sword held high, then he fell forward and off his horse. But the sword flew forward landing point first in the sand and at the feet of Malechar, gleaming gold, shining, gleaming gold. And Malechar knew the horror of what just happened.

King Bathen saw the headless boy fall to the ground, and a sickened feeling swept through his body, as though a massive wave poured down upon him. He seized upon his saddle horn hard to prevent himself from falling off.

Captain Booter felt a wave of bitterness and anger come upon him. This wave seem to pass over the entire army of Eden, and each man drew deep breath after deep breath, clenching teeth and clutching and unclenching hands into fist. Even the horses snorted loudly and pawed and tore at the ground with a quickened violence. Unsheathing his sword, Captain Booter screamed out, "For Prince Abrams and Eden!"

"For Prince Abrams and Eden!" echoed each man as they brought forth their swords.

"EDEN!" screamed Booter.

"EDEN!" the reply echoed louder.

"EDEN!"

"EDEN!"

"EDEN!"

"EDEN!" came the reply again so loudly that villagers down along the coast heard their screams, and young children ran to mothers' arms, and chills swept upon them, for an unknown terror seemed to be carried upon the voices crying out the name ... "EDEN!"

And ten thousand swords shined golden in the sunlight, blazing so brightly that it blinded Malechar and his men to look upon them. And ten thousand men screamed their battle cry as they surged forward as fast as horse and leg could carry them. Each men felt his strength grow with each advancing step. And Malechar felt the terror of this frenzied wave coming towards him, feeling the thundering power, feeling the strength of his men draining as the golden wave majestically in the sun descended upon them.

In one moment, the army of Eden descended upon the soldiers of Malechar. Screaming louder than men have ever screamed in Malechar's memory of battle. The foot soldiers ran as swiftly as Booter's cavalry did in that gap between the armies.

Each man of Eden felt continuous and renewed strength with each yell, with each step, with each swing of the sword and axe. Bravery was commonplace and fighting skill enhanced with the fury of hate and vengeance. The blacksmith, Ian Caulens, snapped his spear thrusting into an enemy after several kills, but he continued advancing by swinging the shaft fiercely upon the enemies' skulls. Pay McCloud, a baker, who was looked upon as a gentle man, lost his sword when it stuck into the backbone of a spearman, and in a frenzy maniacal fury jumped upon an enemy and tore the throat open with his teeth. Such was the power and awful glory of Eden's men at war.

Even the old king found himself being pulled along by his army. Never had he felt such strength in his body, nor felt as one with his horse. His sword glistened with blood as he swung to and fro upon the hated men in black. The thundering mass shook the ground as it swept into its enemy.

The screams of Bathen's men mingled with the dying screams of Malchar's bodyguard as sword thrust against sword and shield. But the power of the golden blades made any attempt to block or thrust away their blows useless. And arms swung their deadly blades unabated until no man of Malechar remained breathing. Shebanja had received blow after blow as several man of Eden passed and loosened their fury upon him. Even Malechar fell to the power of the sword, the sword held by Captain Booter,s hand. And as he fell to his knees mortally wounded, Booter swung his sword upon Malechar's neck, severing the dreaded man's head.

What had seemed an eternity was over in less than a quarter hour. Grasping profusely, the men of Eden walked about the fallen and utterly destroyed army of Malechar. With arms quivering from fatigue, they lifted or rolled over each man to make sure no life remained. And they wondered at the swords of gold that they held in their hands.

Slowly, the awesome power they had drained from them as they put their swords away. And as each man pulled his sword back out of its sheath, it was still shining, but as the silver steel as before the battle. They could only shake their heads in astonishment as they tried to explain the miracle of what just happened. The battlefield was strewn with dead bodies, and none wore the blue of Eden. Here the most feared and deadly force known lay totally annihilated before them.

King Bathen gazed upon the carnage. His Eden was safe. Then his eyes fell upon the small headless body of his young prince. He tried to ride towards it, but grief overcame him, and he turned his horse towards the castle. Slowly he rode towards it, for his Eden was safe, but his heart now felt crushed within him. As exhaustion set in, he felt no joy in his kingdom, no sense in its safety, only pain that his seed was destroyed. He struggled to remain seated and fought to compose himself as the gates to the castle opened before him.

"Soldiers have come ahead speaking of your great victory, my lord," Princess Sara spoke as she ran along his mount. "The people rejoice in your mighty victory and speak of wonder at the miracle of the golden swords."

But the king wearily plodded to the main hall, and Sara sensed a terrible loss. Stammering, he spoke the words of death to her about prince Abrams. As he sat upon the throne, she cast herself down by his side and wailed. The rejoicing court members quickly left the room to these two in their misery. Surely, the miracle had been conceived, and surely, it had asked its price.

After a long time, Captain Booter came into the room but was not alone. "Sire," he spoke. "Your kingdom is safe, and so is your prince."

Slowly, the king looked up. His head jerked back in amazement, and princess Sara shrieked out Abrams name and seized him in her arms.

As the clouded thoughts fled his mind, Bathen looked up at Captain Booter's face to see tears and loss reflected in it, and he understood what had happened.

"Andrew, Our beloved Andrew," Bathen whispered.

"Yes, my lord. It was Andrew dressed as prince Abrams," wept Captain Booter. After a few moments, he spoke again. "He was such a good son. I always impressed upon him to do one's duty was to fulfill one's life. I never thought that doing his duty would cost him his life, not at his age."

Bathen gathered himself up and seized Abrams with hugs and kisses. Then he walked to his loyal captain and embraced him. Before he could talk, Captain Booter spoke. "Forgive me, my king. I do not begrudge the life of prince Abrams. Had we not won today, perhaps in time both lads would have been murdered and everything else destroyed. Andrew did his duty, which was to protect the prince, his friend, no … more like his brother. I am very proud that such a young man could comprehend such responsibility and act upon it. His was a noble death, but still, I can not help my grief either. He was all my treasure, too." The king nodded in agreement and sat back down, speechless to console his friend.

Prince Abrams explained to all how Andrew had knocked him out, tied him up, and went about masquerading as the prince. "It is strange, grandfather," he cried. "Before we fell asleep, I had intended to do exactly the same thing to Andrew. I was not about to let him die for my royal obligation. He was my dear friend, and I shall always miss him."

Then the sound of the front door bursting open quieted everyone. In strode Anasha, visibly shaken from the fatigue of his speedy trip, and from the sense of loss when unable to locate the two boys. "I thought you would be here," he spoke harshly. "Did not your king instruct you to stay with me?"

Timidly, prince Abrams nodded. Then he ran to the physician's arms to be welcomed by his embrace. "I was sick with worry," the old man replied. "I have heard what Andrew did. So! The legend was not false, they usually are not."

He kissed princess Sara on the hands then seized Captain Booter on the shoulders, then continued. "You see, it was said when someone pure of heart and noble in cause took on great evil, a mighty force would come to his aid. It took a young boy to fulfill this act, and in this case, your swords once again became the instruments of this power, and they turned gold by its very purity. That Andrew faced Malechar and gave his life was the catalyst for such a miracle. It was his love of country and duty, his love of prince Abrams here that showed his heart to be good and pure. But the miracle that unfolded this morning surely is a manifestation of its being."

They all remained silent after Anasha spoke. Then Captain Booter bid good day to all, and he left Andrew's body for the last time, and went to see his family. Shortly afterwards, the members of the court returned, and much discussion and rejoicing began.

It was towards evening, the time when dusk is about to be swept across the land, that king Bathen and prince Abrams reached the battleground. All had been gathered up on scores of gigantic pyres that now blazed away. They watched as darkness came, but the fires still roared on, giving the area a great light. Both king and prince walked to the water's edge and gazed towards the continent.

Holding the boy closely, Bathen spoke. "I have not much time left, perhaps a few years. You will have to train hard and long. The people over there will be waiting for us to come and rid them of the remaining tyranny that holds them, guided and driven from Froth. Who knows if there are anymore Malechars awaiting us from that land. Hopefully, it should not be too difficult, for we will face an enemy divided and confused for now. Perhaps we can get to your father in time. But if not, the long hard journey into Froth will call, and by then, you may have to face it and proceed to your destiny. There, a more evil and stronger enemy will await you. Keep your heart pure towards that objective, and then perhaps the miracle of the swords of gold will come again."

Bob Troyer raised his head after reading the last scroll. Kanta sat transfixed, looking into the fire and Nance had tears flowing freely down her face, as did both children who had their heads on her lap. Even Bob sat silent then.

"What a beautiful story," Nance whispered. "What a portion of history unheard of by anyone before us. How the professor will marvel at this saga."

Roger looked up and asked. "Dad, what do you suppose happened afterwards?"

"I don't know, son," he replied. "This asks as many questions as it answered."

Kanta stood up and turned towards them, then spoke. "The answers must lie within the remains of the castle that you mentioned Mr. Lukins found." He then stopped to stoke the flames in the fireplace, then uttered. "My people, my beautiful people. I have always felt you've lived gloriously, now I know."

"What about the castle, honey?" Nance asked Bob. "Do you think any answers lie there?"

"Well, it seems it could be a major piece of the puzzle. But for now, we have a couple days to get back to the continent and the university. Professor Moriarity will be overwhelmed by these scrolls and the story they tell. But with these, I'm positive he'll get the necessary backing needed to proceed with such a search. The remaining secrets must be there. Yes, the castle will tell us more. But that will be another story, another adventures we can all go on."

"He is the heartbeat behind every page of this book. My only son—
God's greatest gift to me and my wife. From the moment he came
into our lives, I never envied another man... because I already had
everything—aside from salvation."

www.ingramcontent.com/pod-product-compliance
Lightning Source LLC
Chambersburg PA
CBHW051218120626
46547CB00013B/1410